Transforming
Early Learners
into Superb Readers

Promoting Literacy at School, at Home, and within the Community

Andrea M. Nelson-Royes

ROWMAN & LITTLEFIELD EDUCATION
A division of
ROWMAN & LITTLEFIELD PUBLISHERS, INC.
Lanham • New York • Toronto • Plymouth, UK

Published by Rowman & Littlefield Education
A division of Rowman & Littlefield Publishers, Inc.
A wholly owned subsidiary of The Rowman & Littlefield Publishing Group, Inc.
4501 Forbes Boulevard, Suite 200, Lanham, Maryland 20706
www.rowman.com

10 Thornbury Road, Plymouth PL6 7PP, United Kingdom

British Library Cataloguing in Publication Information Available

Library of Congress Cataloging-in-Publication Data

Nelson-Royes, Andrea M., 1964-
  Transforming early learners into superb readers : promoting literacy at school, at home, and within the community / Andrea M. Nelson-Royes.
    p. cm.
  Includes bibliographical references.
  ISBN 978-1-61048-872-3 (cloth : alk. paper)—ISBN 978-1-61048-874-7 (electronic)
  1. Reading (Early childhood) 2. Early childhood education—Parent participation. I. Title.
  LB1139.5.R43N45 2012
  372.4—dc23

                                                                    2012026705

Printed in the United States of America

Table of Contents

Foreword

For fifteen years, I was a secondary-level (grades six through twelve) English educator who also taught math. My students usually had literacy levels that were two to three levels below the norm. Over the course of two years, I was able to help my students improve their literacy levels to the point of not only graduating from high school, but also being successful in postsecondary pursuits.

At the secondary level, the tacit assumption is that adolescents already know the basics of reading, that they know how to use phonetics and decoding processes to understand text. With my students, however, these skills weren't evident. From time to time, I wondered why these students didn't learn the fundamentals of literacy in their early childhood and elementary years. Was it because their previous educators didn't have the tools and skills, or was it because they didn't have the extra time to spend on "slow" students? Those questions were quickly dismissed, because my goal was to prepare students for academic adulthood, so I focused only on the present.

As a university professor in teacher education and managing editor of *Illinois Schools Journal*, I have become aware of many aspects of public and parochial education. With my special interest in secondary-level literacy, manuscripts that focus on literacy issues are of interest to me. One of those manuscripts was written by the author of this book, Dr. Andrea Nelson-Royes. Her manuscript helped me determine some possible reasons why my adolescent students lacked basic literacy skills.

Theoretically, text comprises symbols that convey meaning, and that meaning changes according to the context and the perception of the reader. No wonder reading is difficult work. One symbol can have multiple meanings, depending on how it is used. For example, early childhood and elementary-level students may encounter "→" for the first time, and they are taught that it denotes a direction. However, as their education advances, they learn more meanings for this same symbol.

It takes time and energy to identify the symbol, determine its use, and, finally, determine its meaning. These identification and determination skills are taught throughout students' educational career, but they are introduced in the early childhood years. If students do not grasp and understand these literacy skills early in their schooling, they will have serious problems as they advance through their school years. My students had serious literacy problems, for they did not fully understand the reading process when they were young children.

There are a myriad of literacy books, but many of them focus on elementary and secondary-level students. In addition, many of these books use academic language, language that can be inaccessible to the everyday person.

This book takes literacy theory and research and puts it in practical, usable pieces of information. It has the same readability as a newspaper and most trade magazines, so parents and caregivers will be able to understand and apply the information. Within its covers are suggested texts, methodologies, and lists of resources for everyone to use. Not all tools and methods fit all students. The variety of information allows the reader to pick and choose the most effective methods for a particular child.

This book also provides a starting point for educators, parents, and caregivers of all young children. Parents and caregivers want to help their children succeed, but many of these adults feel either insecure or inadequately prepared to help their children. Also, novice educators, although armed with academic knowledge, may have difficulty applying theory, given the classroom realities.

Transforming Early Learners into Superb Readers: Promoting Literacy at School, at Home, and within the Community is easy to understand and provides salient information for all stakeholders in the education of young readers. With practical information that is supported by research and theory, it is a nice companion to a literacy textbook or a parenting handbook.

Byung-In Seo, PhD
associate professor, Chicago State University
managing editor, *Illinois Schools Journal*

Preface

*T*ransforming *Early Learners into Superb Readers: Promoting Literacy at School, at Home, and within the Community* aids elementary educators, reading specialists, school administrators, private and public educators, parents, and caregivers who want to help early learners become proficient readers. All these individuals can play considerable roles in developing a child's reading readiness. It is therefore essential that a collaborative effort exist among them in order for children to obtain a high-quality education.

The early years are the most important for children, because they are the formative years, so it is vital for children to build a solid reading foundation when they are most receptive. Foremost, all children need to grow up healthy and joyful; they must also develop reading skills to support overall intellectual development. How well children read affects not only how successful they are in school, but also how well they perform throughout their lives. No other skill imparted in school and learned by children is more vital than reading. Reading is the entryway to all other knowledge.

One of the most exhilarating teaching experiences in the world is aiding your own child to make his or her first tentative strides on the path to becoming an accomplished reader. A great deal of research has been done about how children learn to read, but nothing guarantees that children will become readers without experiencing some difficulty. At times there may be ups and downs; however, the superb news is that providing the underpinning for children to become proficient readers is one of the most fulfilling roles for educators, parents, and caregivers. To be successful in school, children must have someone who truly cares about their welfare, whether it is an educator, parent, or caregiver.

All children have tremendous potential and ability. I helped my daughter, Natalie, who was struggling to learn to read. I believed my daughter could achieve more with help and encouragement. The child's success resulted from a collaborative effort among my daughter's first-grade teacher, my daughter, and me. Helping Natalie learn to read was a delight. It afforded me the opportunity to spend more time in personal, close, and exhilarating contact with her. Assisting Natalie turned out to be one of the most rewarding experiences of my life, because it allowed me to watch her develop and progress as a skilled reader with ease and confidence. I especially glow with pride when I observe her open and turn the pages of a book with enthusiasm and joy.

Learning how to read is crucial to every child, and all children must learn to read before they get frustrated, feel hopeless, or quit. Most of the time, a child's reading success is attributed to someone who was involved in his or her education. By helping early learners to read, adults launch a legacy that will stay with children for the rest of their lives. It is therefore crucial to begin early and foster a lifelong love of reading, thus furnishing children with the skills they require to be successful. Concerned adults who understand what can hinder children's reading success are better able to evaluate children's requirements, weigh children's learning support alternatives, and monitor children's progress.

I urge all adults in the life of a child—educators, parents, and caregivers—to relish every minute of transforming an early learner into a superb reader.

Acknowledgments

Nobody ever writes a book all by himself or herself. Behind every work is a list of individuals who made it achievable. Thank you to everyone who has helped with this book. My warmest thanks to my family. I want to express my sincere appreciation for your support.

Many thanks to my editor, Bobbie Christmas, at Zebra Communications; Mary McMenamin, the assistant editor at Rowman & Littlefield Education; Dr. Tom Koerner, vice president and editorial director at Rowman & Littlefield Education; and Dr. Byung-In Seo, associate professor of education, Department of Doctoral Studies, Chicago State University, and managing editor of the *Illinois Schools Journal*. Thanks to all of you for your time spent reviewing and editing this book.

Finally, I owe my parents a huge debt of gratitude for allowing me to develop the wisdom to work arduously to accomplish what I desired, wisdom that has remained with me throughout my life. I sincerely extend heartfelt appreciation to all.

Introduction

Children want to learn to read, can learn to read, are learning to read, and must learn to read, yet reading underachievement plagues children across the nation. The National Assessment of Educational Progress (NAEP) reveals that more than one-third of fourth graders fail to attain basic levels of reading achievement. Essentially, reading is about deciphering shapes on a sheet or screen to reveal subtle meanings. Learning to read in early years is crucial to every child's success.

There is little reservation about the benefits of involving parents in their children's schooling. Endeavoring to educate children without parental help and support is like raking leaves in a high wind. Parents are a child's earliest and most influential educators. Schools that fail to take parents' influence into account make teaching children to read much more difficult.

The constraints of time and opportunity make it difficult for educators to provide all the help necessary for struggling children, so a strong partnership among educators, parents, and caregivers is crucial to providing a high-quality education to children. Working together, these people strengthen each other's efforts. Without this collaboration, neither educators nor parents nor caregivers are completely successful alone. Ultimately, schools need parents and caregivers, and parents and caregivers need schools.

Children need confidence if they are to learn to read; and numerous educators, parents, and caregivers will confirm that reading failure destroys a child's self-confidence and motivation to learn long term. Reading failure causes frustration and behavioral problems that lead to a downward spiral in achievement. Reading failure demoralizes a child and destroys his or her self-image. Out of shame, a disheartened reader may endeavor to conceal his or her deficiency, avoid reading aloud, and shun chances to practice reading at home. Without extra practice and intervention, a young reader slips further and further behind.

Transforming Early Learners into Superb Readers: Promoting Literacy at School, at Home, and within the Community provides educators, parents, and caregivers with information to help children develop into superb lifelong readers, and children will foster a love of books from an early age. In this book, educators, parents, and caregivers will find the answers to the following questions and more:

- How do children become proficient (defined by federal law as a fixed level of ability that all children can attain) lifelong readers?
- What information do we need to advance children's reading efforts?
- What works in helping struggling readers learn to read?
- What reading programs are effective, and when should they be implemented?
- Can we support children's reading efforts through collaboration between school and home?

This book is organized into five chapters:

Chapter 1, Transforming Early Learners into Superb Readers, reveals the importance of reading; the reading challenges that children different from the mainstream face; uncovering how to teach children to read successfully; learning to read; what early readers need to be taught to become superb readers; and the development stages of early readers.

Chapter 2, Developing a Balanced Teaching Strategy and Teaching Struggling Readers, discusses phonics versus whole-language; reading aloud; shared reading; guided reading; independent reading; identifying and nurturing the struggling reader; and what educators, parents, and caregivers must do to seek help for struggling readers.

Chapter 3, Engaging Readers through Books and Technology, covers using the library; technology and learning with computers; technology and the building blocks for teaching early learners to read; technology and early learners' motivation; as well as lesson plans incorporating reading and technology.

Chapter 4, Learning to Read and Reading to Learn: Children's Literature, introduces the best children's books for early learners, contained in the appendixes section; and defines the following types of children's literature: picture books, easy reader books, chapter books, nonfiction books, fiction books, traditional literature books, biography books, and poetry books.

Chapter 5, Encouraging Children to Love What They Read, ends with professional development and Literacy First, a type of professional development for educators; roles of reading specialists; children's motivation to read; early intervention programs; supplemental comprehensive intervention reading programs; and action steps for educators.

Each chapter ends with a Points to Remember section that reflects the concepts of the topic. The appendixes, presented in an easy-to-understand format, include high-frequency words 1–100; lists of 300 instant sight words; the alphabet chart; digraph and blend sounds charts; silent *E* chart; a list of educational literacy websites; Newbery Medal books (1922–2012); Caldecott Medal books (1938–2012); and resources on literacy and reading for everyone to use.

Learning to read—or read better—must be perceived as a child's exploration to discover meaning from the page as the words connect to something in each child's range of knowledge. This book provides information for educators, who are encouraged to share the book with parents and caregivers. Together all must work as a team to help children excel at reading and nurture a love of reading. Helping a child learn to read is a gift that will last a lifetime, and it takes a partnership among all concerned individuals.

1

📖

Transforming Early
Learners into Superb Readers

This chapter reveals the importance of reading, the reading challenges those children different from the mainstream face, uncovering how to teach children to read successfully, learning to read, what early readers need to be taught to become superb readers, and the development stages of early readers.

THE IMPORTANCE OF READING

Reading represents a fundamental skill, and its achievement is the foundation of all learning, as well as a major objective of schools. Children who are inefficient readers suffer cumulative deficiency across many content areas that require reading skills as a prerequisite. Children cannot master language arts, mathematics, science, social studies, art, or music without a solid foundation in reading fluency and vocabulary. All subjects require children to be able to read and comprehend the subject matter.

The National Center for Education, the primary federal entity for collecting and analyzing data related to education, released in November 2011 the "Nation's Report Card: Reading 2011." This report indicated the literacy skills of our nation's fourth-grade students, as measured by the National Assessment of Educational Progress (NAEP). A nationally representative sample was taken of about 213,100 fourth graders from about 7,590 schools. The schools that participated in the 2011 NAEP reading analysis were public schools (including charter schools), private schools, Bureau of Indian Education schools, and Department of Defense Schools.

The report indicated that about 67 percent of fourth graders performed at or above the basic level in 2011. The other 33 percent of fourth graders performed at or above proficient level, of which only 8 percent performed at an advanced level. The average reading score in 2011 was unchanged from the previous report released in March 2010, when a representative sample was taken of more than 178,000 fourth graders who participated in the 2009 NAEP reading analysis. The national results from the 2011 reading assessment were compared to nine previous assessment years at grade four. Results from the NAEP reveal that more than one-third of America's fourth graders read at levels so low they cannot complete their schoolwork successfully. The results are disturbing and indicate that many children are leaving their early years and entering fourth grade at or below basic level.

Basic level denotes partial mastery of prerequisite knowledge and skills that are fundamental for proficient work at each grade. Children at the basic level must be able to locate relevant information, make simple inferences, and use their understanding of text to identify details that support a given interpretation or conclusion.

Proficient level represents solid academic performance. Children reaching this level must have demonstrated competency over challenging subject matter. Children at the proficient level must be able to integrate and interpret texts and apply their understanding of the text to draw conclusions and make evaluations.

Advanced level signifies superior performance. Children at the advanced level must be able to make complex inferences and build and support their inferential understanding of the text. In addition, children must be able to apply their understanding of a text to make and support a judgment.

The following are the examples and skills noted by the National Center of Education that fourth graders demonstrated at each achievement level for the previous assessment years:

1. Basic level. Know how to interpret a character's statement to describe a character trait.
2. Proficient level. Recognize the main problem that a character encounters in a story.
3. Advanced level. Use story events to support an opinion about story type.

Data from the NAEP further indicated that insufficient reading skills of children could lead to higher school dropout rates, more out-of-wedlock pregnancies, drug abuse, and crime. As those dropout children become adults, they will exhibit poorer reading skills, experience trouble finding well-paying steady jobs, and undergo a more difficult time attaining further education. Dropouts generally face a life of failure and futility, a life in which they draw more from society than they contribute to it.

As society becomes more technically and socially complex, early learners must not miss out on the fundamentals of reading that enable them to become skilled readers. The costs, in terms of lost intellectual potential and increased rates of emotional and behavioral problems, are too high.

Overall, the majority of educators, parents, and caregivers concur that reading is the most important subject for children to learn. It is therefore imperative that educators, in a collaborative effort with parents and caregivers, teach every child to read and steer clear of the harmful consequences associated with academic failure.

A literate or superb reader is defined as a child who is a proficient reader. Children who are proficient early readers tend to find pleasure and enjoyment in reading. Conversely, children who are slow at learning to read and who fall behind their peers are more likely to find that reading is a chore, not a pleasure. Consequently, they fail to get as much practice as their peers. Such children do not learn to cope with more difficult texts on their own, as their peers do, and as a result, they fall further and further behind academically. Furthermore, children who read less have limited vocabulary growth, and consequently their reading development is that much more inhibited.

When children learn to read, they attain the essentials for unlocking the door to knowledge. Without this skill, they linger behind their more advancing peers who are reading. One of the most important things that educators, parents, and caregivers can do for children is help them develop their reading skills. Too few children receive effective support. Children are more inclined to succeed in learning when educators, parents, and caregivers actively support their children and read to them.

READING CHALLENGES FOR CHILDREN DIFFERENT FROM THE MAINSTREAM

More than forty years ago, legendary sociologist James Coleman found that the socioeconomic status of a child's family was the biggest predictor of educational achievement. Statistics reveal the sad state of family life and the problems facing children in today's economy. There are high divorce rates, numerous single-parent homes or those with two working parents, increasing teenage pregnancies, and children from homes that have cultural and linguistic backgrounds that are different from the mainstream. These situations all create obstacles to successful schooling and parenting. Sadly, many children from these families are worried about the demands and disruptions of their life. Moreover, their parents may be unable to devote enough time and effort to help their children. Often the adults do not know how to help their children with schoolwork or how to foster a positive attitude toward learning.

According to the U.S. Census Bureau (2009), the nation's minority population on July 1, 2008, was 104.6 million, or 34 percent of the total population. Minorities are defined as any group other than single-race, non-Hispanic white. The Census Bureau further revealed that 47 percent of American children under the age of five are born to minority groups. On the whole, our nation's population growth is fastest among minorities.

Not all children enter school equally prepared to learn to read, and those from the nation's most economically disadvantaged families are the least likely to be well prepared to succeed. The incidence of reading failure is particularly high within low-income families, ethnic minority groups, and English-language learners. Educators face challenges when teaching children from low-income families, ethnic minority groups, and English-language learners' households; nevertheless, whatever the economic, racial, or cultural backgrounds, parents and caregivers have expectations for their children to be successful in school. School-parent partnerships have resulted in empowering parents to take an active role in the education of their children, leading to higher levels of school achievement independent of the economic, racial, or cultural background of the family.

Schools need to work with families to improve the home learning environment, and educators need to initiate this involvement. The types of classified parent involvement include the following:

- Basic support for the child as a learner
- School-home communications
- Involvement at school
- Participation in decision making, governance, and advocacy
- Taking part in learning activities at home

The primary way educators involve parents in their children's development is through monitoring homework.

Particular attention must be given to children who are likely to need the most help. These children are commonly the ones who have learning disabilities, limited English proficiency, or other challenges that make the children different from the mainstream. These children need high, but realizable, aspirations established through a collaborative effort by educators, parents, caregivers, and any specialists. Most children with disabilities or disadvantages learn to read in much the same way as other children, even though they may require much more time and intensive help. With educators, parents, caregivers, and specialists working together, however, these children can meet their goals.

UNCOVERING WAYS TO TEACH
CHILDREN TO READ SUCCESSFULLY

On January 8, 2002, President George W. Bush signed the No Child Left Behind Act (NCLB) into law. This legislation represented his education-reform plan and contained the most sweeping changes to the Elementary and Secondary Education Act since its enactment in 1965. One of the primary intents of NCLB was to increase the number of children reading on grade level by the end of third grade. Although there are no easy solutions that improve reading success, the information base shows the skills children must learn to read well. These skills become the basis of curriculum decisions and instruction to prevent the predictable consequences of early reading failure.

An extensive body of reading research has resulted in a great deal of information about the knowledge and skills essential for becoming a proficient reader. Across the field of research on reading, undeniable evidence shows a strong relationship between word recognition and reading comprehension. In addition, the vast majority of low-progress readers demonstrate deficits in their phonological processing skills and need remediation to detect, access, manipulate, and relate sounds and codes, such as the letters and words of language.

Researchers have uncovered how to teach children to read successfully. In 2000, The National Reading Panel (NRP), the largest, most comprehensive congressionally mandated independent panel, issued a report to help educators, parents, and caregivers identify key skills and methods central to reading achievement. This panel was charged with reviewing research in reading instruction. Its focus was on the critical years of kindergarten through third grade. The panel reviewed more than 100,000 studies in the United States and Europe.

The findings concluded that for children to become literate, they must learn the following five components of effective reading instruction:

1. Phonemic awareness is the ability to hear, identify, and manipulate the individual sounds in spoken words.
2. Phonics is the relationship between the letters of the written language and the sounds of spoken language.
3. Vocabulary development refers to the words children must know to read effectively.
4. Reading fluency is the ability to read text accurately and quickly with expression.
5. Reading comprehension is the competence to understand and gain meaning from what has been read.

Although no easy answers or quick solutions exist for boosting reading achievement, an extensive foundation exists to point out the techniques that children must learn in order to read well. Teaching children to read is one of the most investigated areas of education; however, researchers still cannot state precisely how children learn to read, because reading is a complex skill. Also, all children come to school with a wide range of ability levels and are individuals who learn in different ways.

The methods of teaching children to read are varied across districts, schools, and classrooms. Educators must endeavor to team up with parents and caregivers and inform them of how their child is being taught to read and how they can best support their child's reading efforts at home. Special programs and remediation approaches must be used to assist children in improving their reading skills, to help children foster an appreciation for reading as a lifelong hobby.

LEARNING TO READ

Learning to read is a challenge for about 40 percent of all children. With early intervention, though, many reading problems can be remediated. Unfortunately, 44 percent of parents and caregivers who detect their child may be having difficulty reading wait a year or more before seeking help (Reading Rockets, 2012). As the child becomes older, it becomes more difficult to teach him or her to read. If a child cannot read well by the end of third grade, it will be very challenging for the child to attain grade-level proficiency, which has devastating effects on a child's academic progress. About half of all children will learn to read regardless of how they are taught.

The ability to read is undeniably critical to success in today's society. It paves the way for success in school, which builds self-confidence and motivates children to set high expectations for life. Learning to read proficiently is the target of effective instruction for children in kindergarten through third grade; therefore, these years present the best opportunity for a child to become a proficient reader.

Children below the age of five can understand remarkable quantities of information. Most children learn to read with some proficiency between the ages of about five years old and seven years old, by the end of first grade. A failure to make even a modest beginning in reading skill by the age of seven places a child at educational risk. Much learning depends on the ability to read, and poor readers are less likely to receive appropriate academic intervention when they become older.

When children acquire the fundamentals of reading, little by little, they build the knowledge that is needed for being a proficient reader. Over their first six years, most children do the following:

- Talk and listen to conversations
- Listen to stories read aloud
- Pretend that they are reading
- Discover how to handle books by turning the pages by themselves
- Learn about print and how it works
- Recognize letters by name and shape
- Identify separate sounds in spoken language
- Write with scribbles and drawing
- Join single letters with the sounds they make
- Link what they already know to what they hear and read
- Guess what comes next in stories and poems
- Join combinations of letters with sounds
- Distinguish simple words in print
- Summarize the plot of a story
- Write individual letters of the alphabet
- Print words
- Compose simple sentences
- Read simple books
- Write to communicate

It is critical to start early if children are to develop the skills they need to be successful.

Research confirms the strong connection between early skill development and later reading success. Reading is not a skill that is mastered in a few weeks or even few months, though. It is a process that continues throughout a child's school years and over time must lead to independent reading and fluency. Educators, parents, and caregivers need to be aware that not all children learn at the same pace, and that some children might require extra help. The key is to be mindful of a child's reading level so that books and activities are selected that help the child progress.

WHAT EARLY READERS NEED TO KNOW

Identifying Letters, New Words, and Letter Sounds

To help children decipher the code of written language is to help them recognize the relationships between individual letters and the combinations of letters and the sounds they create. When words are in print, they are made of letters, smaller components added together to create the word. Most children must be able to identify most uppercase and lower-case letters accurately by the end of first grade. The exceptions are *b* and *d* or *p, g,* and *q,* which children are still likely to confuse or reverse as late as second grade.

One of the most important skills learned by first grade is the identification of the sounding-out strategy known as phonics. Knowledge of letter-sound relationships is necessary to "phonologically recode," or look at the letters of a word and convert them into the appropriate sound. Literate readers will predict what the text might say, which helps a child to become a better reader. A component of learning to read is learning the expected letter-sound patterns in written words. Consequently, these letter sounds help a child decipher written words into the sounds of the spoken language they symbolize. Children must understand that letters have names, represent sounds, and have dissimilar shapes, and that letters make words that create different meanings.

Educators must communicate with parents and caregivers about how they introduce letters into the classroom to children. Educators also need to inform parents and caregivers to use their child's homework and handouts as a guide to help their children at home. Indeed, parents and caregivers are the key factors of family literacy for early-reading learners.

Sight Words

Sight-word learning is a connection-forming process. Connections are formed that link spellings of written words to their pronunciations and meanings in memory. A sight word is simply a word that can be instantly recognized by a quick look at the configuration of letters. It is necessary for children to gain a growing list of words they identify with ease, which enables them to become fluent readers. Reading a word four to fourteen times secures its connection in memory.

Educators generally focus on two types of sight words. The first type is made up of commonly used words. The second type of sight words is composed of words that cannot be deciphered in isolation. If a child is familiar with letter sounds, he or she will most likely read a word by blending the letter sounds. Some words do not follow the rules of phonics; therefore, it is essential to teach a child these words in the early phase of reading. Once children commit the following thirty-three words to memory, they are on their way to becoming better readers: *a, of, and, that, he, the, I, to, in, was, it, all, had, said, as, have, so, at, him, they, be, his, we, but, not, with, are, on, you, for, one, she,* and *her.*

Educators must provide parents and caregivers with a list of the thirty-three words for their children to commit to memory. Further, educators must stress ways for parents and caregivers to help their children commit these words to memory, such as writing or saying them daily until they are memorized. Children also identify printed words in the environment. These words become a central and crucial part of learning to read. Parents and caregivers who read with their children assist educators in helping their children develop their skills of decoding, understanding, and learning sight words and sounds.

Appendix A contains the list of high-frequency words 1–100, and appendix B contains lists of 300 instant sight words. Research indicates that 100 high-frequency words must be learned by children each year in the primary grades. If memorized, children are able to identify at least the lists of 300 instant words, which comprise up to two-thirds of elementary reading materials by the completion of the third grade.

Phonics

Phonics education plays an important role in deciphering. The objective of phonics is to help children learn and draw on the alphabetic principle. *Alphabetic* refers to the abilities required to decipher print to speech, which is the relationship between letters and sounds. Knowledge of these associations helps children identify familiar words accurately and automatically and decipher new words. See appendix C for an alphabet chart.

Phonics can be taught explicitly or implicitly. Explicit phonics entails telling children directly the sounds of individual letters. Implicit phonics encourages children to make the sounds that correspond to letters from accumulated auditory and visual exposure to words containing those letters. Educators must blend these techniques for children to learn how to decipher words.

Phonics instruction basically teaches children the relationships between the look of the letters (graphemes) of written language and the individual sounds (phonemes) of spoken language. It also teaches children to apply these relationships when reading words. Some educators, parents, and caregivers believe that phonics is the key to learning how to read. To develop a child's skill in phonics and phonemic awareness, educators need to adhere to the following practices and share this information with parents and caregivers:

1. Encourage children to write and spell words. Practice spelling words together often, because spelling words aloud or in writing helps children learn phonics.
2. Have fun with rhymes. Rhyming words give children ample practice in learning word families. Word families are groups of words that have a common feature or pattern. They have the same combinations of letters in them and a similar sound. For example, *at, cat, fat, hat,*

and *sat* are a family of words with the common *"at"* sound and letter combination.

3. Demonstrate to children how to blend letters to sound out words.
4. Teach the *h* digraphs: *ch, sh, th, wh, ph,* and *gh.* Digraphs are two letters that, when placed side by side, can make a completely different sound from the sounds typical of the individual letters. See appendix D for digraph chart and blend sounds.
5. Teach the silent *e* rule, one of the most frequently used rules. When a word has a vowel, a consonant, and a final *e,* the silent *e* makes the vowel say its name. For example, if a silent *e* is added to the end of a word with just one consonant as the last letter, the vowel in the middle of the word changes its sound; however, it happens only if the word ends with just one consonant. For instance, the word *can* ends with just one consonant, so when you add a silent *e* to the end of *can,* it changes the sound of the vowel *a,* and the word becomes *cane.* On the other hand, if a word ends with more than one consonant, then the vowel in the middle does not change its sound, such as *back, fill,* and *pass.* See appendix E for a silent E chart.
6. Help children understand r-controlled vowel sounds. These are vowels followed by the consonant *r: ar, er, ir, or, ur.* Notice that *er, ir,* and *ur* can make similar sounds. The *r* causes a change in the pronunciation of the vowel. For example, *ar: car, star, arm, barn; er: sister, brother, waiter, barber; ir: girl, bird, shirt, skirt; or: corn, fork, cord, horse;* and *ur: church, nurse, curve,* and *burger.*
7. Teach the ending *ing.* Children must be able to look at this three-letter word fragment and pronounce the *ing* sound. For example: *king, ring, sing,* and *wing.*
8. Explore long-vowel combinations: *ea, ee, ai, ue.* For example, *ea: eat, tea, sea, read; ee: see, peek, queen, sleep; ai: aim, rain, tail, paint;* and *ue: cue, glue, clue, blue.* Children must be taught to remember several long-vowel combinations. For the combinations of letters listed above, the first vowel says its name and the second vowel is silent. Some combinations are exceptions to the rule, such as *ou: you, soul, soup,* and *group; oi: oil, coin, point, voice;* and *oo: zoo, moon, food,* and *baboon.*
9. Explore syllabication. Syllabication is the method of dividing words into syllables (or word parts). Research indicates that children generally use sounds to determine syllable division. Children divide words into parts to decipher them. When children are taught the basic rules in syllabication, it helps them decipher words by recognizing patterns and helps them break down unknown words as a way to recognize them. With practice, children eventually are able to quickly select areas in a word that break into syllables.

Systematic and explicit phonics education improves each child's word recognition, spelling, and reading comprehension. Letters symbolize sounds, and to read words, children have to gain the knowledge of how letters and sounds relate. Research reveals that about two years of phonics instruction is satisfactory for most children. If phonics teaching starts early in kindergarten, it must be concluded by the end of first grade. If it starts at the beginning of first grade, it must be completed by the end of second grade.

Parents and caregivers can help their children learn phonics by using commercially published materials and programs intended explicitly for phonics practice. A collaborative process must exist with a child's educator, however, to avoid confusion with whatever the child is learning at school.

Phonemic Awareness

Effective phonics education is built on a strong foundation of phonemic awareness. Phonemic awareness improves children's word reading and reading comprehension, and it can be used to predict how well children will learn to read. Even though phonemic awareness is a commonly used term in reading, it is often misinterpreted. One misinterpretation is that phonemic awareness and phonics are the same thing, but the two names must not be used interchangeably.

Phonemic awareness is the ability to hear and manipulate the sounds in spoken words, and the understanding that sounds of spoken language work together to make words. Phonics helps children learn the relationship between letters of the written language and the sounds of the spoken language. Put simply, phonemic awareness is auditory and does not involve words in print. If children are to benefit from phonics, however, they need phonemic awareness.

Another misunderstanding about phonemic awareness is that it means the same as phonological awareness. The two names are not interchangeable. Phonemic awareness is a subcategory of phonological awareness. The focus of phonemic awareness is narrow and identifies and manipulates the individual sounds in words. Children who have phonemic awareness skills are likely to have an easier time learning to read, in contrast to children who have not yet mastered any of these skills. Early readers must be aware of how the sounds in each word work before they learn to read print. It is essential for them to recognize that words consist of speech sounds, or phonemes.

Scientific research on phonemic awareness reveals that it

1. may be taught and learned. It allows children to discern, contemplate, and work with sounds in spoken language.

2. helps children learn to read and improves their ability to read words and their reading comprehension.
3. helps children learn to spell by segmenting words into phonemes. Further, phonemic awareness helps children recognize that sounds and letters are interrelated in a predictable way.
4. is most helpful when children are taught to manipulate phonemes by using the letters of the alphabet. Teaching sounds along with the letters of the alphabet helps children notice how phonemic awareness relates to their reading.
5. is most valuable when the focal point is merely on one or two types of phoneme manipulation, rather than on numerous types, which minimizes misunderstanding.

The NRP, in a meta-analysis of phonemic awareness studies, linked phonemic awareness to increased success in reading and spelling for early learners in preschool, kindergarten, and first grade. A meta-analysis is a subset of systematic reviews, a method for systematically combining pertinent qualitative (deals with description) and quantitative (deals with numbers) study data from several selected studies to develop a single conclusion that has greater statistical power. This conclusion is statistically stronger than the analysis of any single study, because of the increased numbers of subjects, greater diversity among subjects, or accumulated effects and results.

Educators, parents, and caregivers must be mindful that a thorough education in phonemic awareness is essential for all early learners to learn to read, particularly children who possess early reading difficulties. Educators need to educate parents and caregivers on ways to aid their children in their development of phonemic awareness. Educators can provide parents and caregivers with a number of age-appropriate activities in blending and segmenting words. When parents and caregivers give children opportunities to experiment with language at home, they increase the chances that their child will develop phonemic awareness with ease at school.

Vocabulary Learning

The size of a child's vocabulary is a strong predictor of reading success, and a large vocabulary is essential in learning to read and for reading comprehension. By the end of first grade, effective readers are exposed to an average of 18,681 words, as opposed to poor readers, who are exposed to an average of 9,975 words. In addition, effective readers have more print exposure to words than poor readers, as they increase with each grade.

Vocabulary can be classified as oral or reading vocabulary. Oral vocabulary refers to words that individuals use in speaking or words that individuals identify in listening. Reading vocabulary refers to words identified or used in print. Children use the words that they have heard to make sense of the words they notice in print.

The following are the four types of vocabulary:

1. Listening vocabulary consists of the words children must identify in order to comprehend what they hear.
2. Speaking vocabulary refers to the words children use when they speak.
3. Reading vocabulary comprises the words children must identify to comprehend what they read.
4. Writing vocabulary is made up of the words children use in writing.

A well-rounded vocabulary is vital in helping children become superb readers, because it enables them to understand words as they read. The single most important activity that educators, parents, and caregivers must do to improve children's vocabulary is to get them to read more. Providing children with different types of texts and different levels of difficulty is beneficial in building children's vocabulary.

Different types of texts and varying levels of difficulty can be used to accomplish several purposes to meet various children's needs. By matching text types with children's reading development, educators are better able to support children's reading progress. The variations in the types of text are greatest at the beginning reading level. Each type of text must be used for any type of reading experiences, such as reading aloud, shared reading, guided reading, and independent reading, which will be discussed in the following chapter. Some types of texts are more suitable for some purposes than others, but all texts can be used for a variety of types of reading. Most important is that children must have a variety of types of text for reading in order to keep them motivated, successful readers.

Reading Fluency

Gaining meaning from text is dependent upon fluent reading. Reading fluency is the bridge that links word recognition and comprehension. Educators, parents, and caregivers must help children become fluent readers by providing them with models of fluent reading by reading aloud to the children and having them continually read passages with assistance.

When children take note of role models of fluent reading, they learn how a reader's tone helps written text make sense. Equally important is having children reread the text once it has been modeled. The text must be moderately easy and include words that children decipher effortlessly. Likewise, the text must be reasonably brief, possibly 50 to 200 words, depending on the child's independent reading level. When a text is at a child's independent reading level, it can be read with about 95 percent accuracy, or misinterpreted roughly only one of every twenty words.

Fluency develops as a result of numerous chances to practice reading with a high degree of success. Fluent readers use a number of methods concurrently to turn script into meaning. Children's fluency is enhanced as they increase their vocabulary. When readers struggle through a text in an effort to decipher words, they lose comprehension. Educators, parents, and caregivers must be aware that repeatedly reading out loud to children provides a model for their oral readings and fluency.

Reading Comprehension

Comprehension is considered the most important aspect of reading. To read with clear comprehension, children need a variety of interrelated skills. On the most basic reading level, children must be capable of deciphering and making sense out of words. After succeeding past the basic deciphering skills, children encounter added challenges. They must be able to understand, recall, and apply what they read. The shift from deciphering words to comprehending information may be particularly complex for some children, including those with learning disabilities.

The following six strategies have a firm scientific basis for improving text comprehension in kindergarten through third-grade children:

1. Monitoring comprehension. Children who are able to monitor their comprehension identify when they do or do not recognize what they read. Children have strategies to "set up" problems in their understanding as problems arise. Instruction in the early grades helps children become better at monitoring their comprehension.
2. Using graphic and semantic organizers. Graphic organizers demonstrate concepts and interrelationships among concepts in a text using diagrams or other pictorial devices. Graphic organizers are known by different names; for instance, maps, webs, graphs, charts, frames, or clusters. These organizers help readers focus on concepts and how they are related to concepts. In addition, they help children read to learn from informational text in the content areas, such as science and social studies. Semantic organizers are graphic organizers that look somewhat like a spider web. In a semantic organizer, lines connect a central concept to a variety of related ideas and events.
3. Recognizing story structure. Story structure refers to the manner in which the content and events of a story are structured into a

plot. Children who identify story structure have better admiration, understanding, and remembrance of stories. In story-structure instruction, children learn to identify the categories of content (such as setting, initiating events, goals, and outcomes) and how this content is organized into a plot. Frequently children learn to recognize story structure through the use of story maps. Story maps are a type of graphic organizer that shows the sequence of events in simple stories.

4. Summarizing is a combination of the important ideas in a text. Children decide what is essential in what they are reading, condense the information, and put it into their own words. A summary is a synthesis of the important ideas in a text.

5. Cooperative learning. Children work together as partners or in small groups on clearly defined tasks. Educators help children learn to work in groups, offer demonstrations of the comprehension approaches, and check the academic development of children. Cooperative learning instruction successfully teaches comprehension strategies in content-area subjects. Children work together to understand content-area texts, helping each other learn and apply comprehension strategies. Content-area texts are selected because they are written to inform and are mainly concerned with the presentation of factual material. Besides technical and specialized vocabulary, most contain format and organizational features that are not found in other materials, especially those used during developmental reading instruction.

6. Effective instruction helps readers use comprehension strategies flexibly and in combination. Research indicates that although it is helpful to provide children with instruction in individual comprehension strategies, proficient readers must be able to coordinate and adjust several strategies to assist comprehension.

In addition, educators, parents, and caregivers can have children build upon their earlier knowledge and understanding to help them comprehend what they are reading. Before the children read the text, educators and helpers need to preview it with them and ask questions pertaining to what the children know about the topic, the concept, or the time period of the selection. They must be asked what knowledge they have about the author. There must be a discussion about the key vocabulary used in the text. Additionally, they must be shown pictures or diagrams to prepare them for what they are about to read.

Mental imagery is also essential. When children create mental images, they engage in text in ways that are personal and memorable to them. Anchored in prior knowledge, images come from emotions and all five senses, which enhance understanding and immerse children in rich detail. It is an experience that, on most occasions, significantly resembles the experience of visualizing some object, event, or scene, but occurs when the relevant object, event, or scene is not actually present to the senses.

One way to help children notice the connections they make to the words on a page is to let them draw while they listen to someone read aloud. Through guided visualization, children learn how to create mental pictures as they read. Early readers who visualize during reading understand and remember what they read better than readers who do not visualize. By using prior knowledge and background experiences, early readers connect the writing in the text with a personal picture. When early learners find that using comprehension strategies helps them learn, they are more likely to be inspired to become more actively involved in learning to read.

DEVELOPMENT STAGES OF EARLY READERS

During preschool, children need to be in an awareness-and-exploration stage, whereby they are exploring their environment and building the groundwork for learning to read. In kindergarten, children must still be in an exploration stage, in which they are developing the fundamental concepts of print and starting to experiment with reading.

In first grade, children must be at an early reading stage, whereby they are progressing toward reading simple stories. By second grade, they must be at a transitional reading stage, whereby they are beginning to read more fluently. Children in third grade must be at an independent and productive stage, where they continue to refine their reading abilities, and by fourth grade and beyond, they must be at an advanced reading stage.

The following are a few things educators need to share with parents and caregivers to make sure their children accomplish their goals:

- At age three or four: Remember nursery rhymes and play rhyming games.
- At about age four: Acquire information or directions from conversations or books that are read aloud to them.
- At age five: Play and enjoy simple word games in which two or more words start with the same sound. For example, identify all the animals they can visualize that begin with the letter *d*.
- At ages five and six: Show they recognize that spoken words can be broken down into smaller parts. For instance, if a child can notice the word *big* in *bigger* or can change a small part of a word and make a

different word. Or by changing the first sound and letter of *cat*, the child can make *hat, sat, bat, mat,* or *rat.*

Experts stress that learning to read is not a single task but consists of many steps on a developmental continuum. When children are beginning to read, they must focus on letters and sounds, recalling words and meaning. In a collaborative effort, parents and caregivers need to help educators by doing the following:

• Read to their children daily
• Help their children read with a purpose
• Discuss the stories
• Reread preferred books
• Partake in activities that enhance their children's vocabulary
• Persuade their children to read critically
• Expand the quality of the reading experience

Preschool and primary school educators need to evaluate an individual child's growth by setting reasonable goals and allowing individual differences. Reading is a complex skill that can take time and patience. Children learn in a variety of ways and come to school with a varied range of ability levels as well.

Educators, parents, and caregivers in search of books to read to early learners must be sure the books are age appropriate, embrace rich language, and contain rhythm, rhyme, or repetition. These reading selections must include a diversity of culture that reveals not only the child's world but also that of others. Moreover, it is crucial for educators, parents, and caregivers to foster a lifetime love of reading in early learners that will remain with them throughout their lives.

POINTS TO REMEMBER

The ability to read is critical to a child's success in school and later life. Nevertheless, learning to read is a challenge for about 40 percent of all children. With early intervention, though, many reading problems can be remediated. The importance of reading cannot be overemphasized, because it is the one academic area that permeates all other academic subjects. Reading well is at the heart of all learning.

Insufficient reading skills of children could lead to higher school dropout rates, more out-of-wedlock pregnancies, drug abuse, and crime. As children who drop out become adults, they exhibit poorer reading skills, experience trouble finding well-paying steady jobs, and encounter difficulty attaining further education. Dropouts generally face a life of failure and futility, a life in which they draw more from society than they contribute to it.

The National Reading Panel concluded that for children to become literate readers, they must be taught and learn the following five components of effective reading instruction:

1. Phonemic awareness is the ability to hear, identify, and manipulate the individual sounds in spoken words.
2. Phonics is the relationship between the letters of the written language and the sounds of spoken language.
3. Vocabulary development refers to the words children must know in order to read effectively.
4. Reading fluency is the ability to read text accurately and quickly with expression.
5. Reading comprehension is the competence to understand and gain meaning from what has been read.

Children are more likely to succeed in learning to read when they are provided with support from their educators, parents, and caregivers. Although no easy answers or quick solutions exist for optimizing reading success, an extensive foundation exists to point out the techniques that children must learn if they are to read well.

2

📖

Developing a Balanced Teaching Strategy and Teaching Struggling Readers

Numerous children have difficulty building meaning from scholarly books. The issue is often resolved when educators promote interaction and collaboration with the material. A balanced teaching strategy integrates all reading approaches, recognizing that children need to employ multiple strategies to become literate readers. As children progressively gather knowledge and proficiency, they become more independent readers.

A balanced teaching strategy also combines the teaching of phonics and the whole-language approach to help children learn to read. Equally important are reading aloud to children, shared reading, guided reading with small groups, and independent reading. Each has a particular function; nonetheless, they all contribute to make certain that children develop into independent, proficient, and enthusiastic readers.

This chapter discusses phonics versus whole language; reading aloud; shared reading; guided reading; independent reading; identifying and nurturing the struggling reader; and what educators, parents, and caregivers must do to seek help for struggling readers.

PHONICS VERSUS WHOLE LANGUAGE

The dispute over the use of phonics and whole language has taken place for years. Whole language reading education is also acknowledged as the "look-say" or "sight-reading" method. Whole language is a method of teaching children to read by recognizing words as whole pieces of

23

language. In the 1960s and 1970s, it was termed the psycholinguistic approach to reading, and it became the most popular trend of reading education during the 1970s. Since the 1980s, however, there has been a disagreement between supporters of phonics-based reading education and supporters of the whole-language approach.

Most educators in the United States combine phonics with some elements of whole language to teach children to read. Researchers and educators recognized that there must be a balance connecting the two approaches of teaching reading. Although true, the whole-language approach has generated much dialogue and disagreement. Parents and caregivers may hear educators refer to the term "whole language" and question its meaning and implication, so it is essential that educators share with parents and caregivers the fundamentals of whole-language teaching.

Whole language is assumed to be literature based, for the reason that children are expected to learn words by listening to them as educators, parents, and caregivers read stories aloud. Supporters of the whole-language process reason that language is an entire scheme of building meaning with words that function in relation to each other in context. They also strongly disapprove of a basic phonics approach to reading. Some of the dissatisfactions are as follows:

- The English language is not easily gained phonetically and should not be broken down into letters and combinations of letters and deciphered. In addition, too many letters and sounds have exceptions to the rule. Further, a rule has to be interchanged so regularly that it is confusing to some children.
- Phonics does not work for a number of children and has a tendency to create slow, word readers and takes up a large part of first grade.
- The importance of phonics is the mechanics of reading, instead of the thought-getting of reading.
- Reading by the phonics approach has a tendency to be unexciting, because it is not related to actual thinking.

The whole-language method allows children to identify numerous words as effortlessly as they must various letters. Children are provided with complete words in order to focus on meaning. On the other hand, phonics provides words letter by letter.

In teaching whole language, educators must teach fifty to seventy-five words with the sight method by saying the word. A story-method approach is useful. This approach selects key words and examines new words in relation to ones committed to memory. Communication and thoughts are more vital than accuracy and correctness in whole language.

Supporters of the whole-language approach say it works because children learn to read with joy and simplicity; therefore, they become enthusiastic, independent, confident, and lifelong readers.

Supporters of phonetics are persistently critical of the whole-language approach. Their criticisms are as follows:

- The teaching of phonics is an important aspect of beginning reading instruction.
- Whole language delays learning to read and even prevents some children from ever learning to read.
- They are dismayed at the apparent approval of inaccuracy of the whole-language method to attain ease and confidence. They believe that whole language requires a huge mental dictionary to keep track of all of the properties of each word.
- They maintain that whole language is supported by the belief that children do not require rules and structure in order to learn.

Educators, parents, and caregivers need to be mindful that the focal point of whole-language reading education is helping children create meaning from the words they read. Various significant features of whole-language thinking take into account the importance of high-quality literature and center on cultural diversity. Whole-language reading education is noted for generating various prospects for children to read.

Whether something is being read aloud or in the company of other children in small guided groups or independently by educators, parents, and caregivers, children need others to read to them. The whole-language approach has presented problems for children who have reading difficulties. These children need clear approaches to develop their reading skills, such as word deciphering, phonemic awareness, and phonics.

Research has shown that effective readers always use phonics to decipher new words. In 1997, the National Reading Panel conducted a study to resolve the dispute over the long-debated disagreement as to which form of reading education is the finer. In 2000, the panel released its findings, stating that the five components that must be taught in an effective reading program are phonemic awareness, phonics, vocabulary development, reading fluency, and reading comprehension.

Still, viewpoints differ over phonics and the whole-language approach to reading; nevertheless, both are necessary for all children to learn to read. In the best of classrooms, educators use a combination of both methods and an assortment of books. Further, children are told to discover the meaning of words based on their knowledge, prediction, and the sounds the words incorporate.

READING ALOUD

Reading aloud is an essential part of a balanced reading education. Additionally, it is the best approach for educators, parents, and caregivers to help children learn to read and become proficient readers. Reading aloud to children must start at an early age; it will develop into a normal procedure and be easier for children as they develop. Reading aloud to children provides them with a model for fluency. In particular, children will model rhythm, sound, and logic of the written language, which will offer them a sense of how the words are pronounced correctly, how phrases are read with variability, and how punctuation marks are used as guideposts.

Reading aloud to children also provides them with the gift of reading readiness, increasing their vocabulary, sequencing skills, listening skills, and comprehension while building their imagination. Reading aloud to children inspires some of them to want to learn more, and therefore gives them the desire to read independently. The commission examining reading in the United States stated in its report "Becoming a Nation of Readers" that reading aloud to children is the most significant activity parents and caregivers can do to help children acquire the knowledge they need for success in reading.

By combining reading aloud with regular silent reading, many children receive a boost in confidence, interest, and improvement toward reading. Equally important, Jim Trelease, author of *The Read-Aloud Handbook*, stated that children need to be read aloud to from socially appropriate books. These books allow children to become naturally and meaningfully engaged with the stories. Furthermore, when children are engaged in a story, they are more likely to create meaning and explore the reading process.

Reading aloud must be an occurrence free from distractions. Children need to be occupied completely by the listening process. Researchers who study how children learn to listen suggest that children listen at a much higher comprehension level than they read until around the eighth grade. For instance, when books are written at the fourth-grade reading level, even first graders are capable of receiving enjoyment from them. Similarly, many fifth graders receive enjoyment in books written for the seventh-grade reading level. Although true, the subject matter has to remain suitable for the age group.

When children are struggling, reading aloud allows them to take pleasure in books read in the classroom or at home. Schools emphasize reading aloud to children in their primary years, because it helps early learners focus and assists educators in identifying a child's reading difficulties. Educators, parents, and caregivers must make the most of reading aloud to children by doing the following in an atmosphere of relaxation and mere enjoyment:

- Select a book that is pleasurable and create an atmosphere intended for relaxation and pleasure.
- Choose stories with engaging characters and an excellent exchange of ideas.
- Discuss the cover with the child.
- Read the title page, identify the author's name, and read it as printed. If the book is illustrated, read the illustrator's name as well.
- Begin by reading at a normal speed and model the acceptable production of sounds so children grasp the cadence of the story.
- When reading aloud, use enthusiasm and expression, especially as it pertains to the dialogue of different characters.
- Perform parts of the story when feasible and use a sense of humor.
- Engage children in discussion of the story by asking questions and talking to them during pauses. Begin with questions relating to the focus of the book and the prediction of the story's plot.
- Share personal thoughts with children about the story.

Reading aloud to children is worthwhile. Educators must encourage parents and caregivers to read to their children every day. A big mistake is for educators, parents, and caregivers to stop reading aloud to children when they become better able to read independently. Reading aloud is a practice that must continue throughout the grades (Anderson et al., 1985). Reading aloud promotes continual interest in reading and stimulates a pleasure connection between the child and the educator, parents, or caregivers.

Educators must offer guidance to parents and caregivers that when reading aloud to their children, introduce them to literature they might not locate on their own: for example, classic children's stories and poetry. Children will willingly listen to adults read more difficult literature that they cannot read themselves. Also, children are more likely to listen to books they may be able to read but would not choose to. Early learners are more eager to select boldly colored picture books and books that include repetitions and rhymes. These books stimulate early learners' interest and visual mind by encouraging them to partake in the reading experience.

When educators, parents, and caregivers read aloud to children, they are modeling fluent reading, promoting enjoyment and appreciation of children's literature, developing vocabulary knowledge, stimulating and motivating independent reading, and, most important, developing bonds. Parents and caregivers must be guided to reserve read-aloud time at bedtime, because most children are in school and/or day care all day. As little as fifteen minutes a day spent reading aloud to children has a significant effect on their becoming lifelong readers and discovering the importance, enthusiasm, and pleasure of reading. Most grow up with fond memories and attachments to adults who read to them when they were young.

SHARED READING

Shared reading is a means for teaching children to read and for teaching children about reading. Shared reading is an interactive reading experience that occurs when children join in or share the reading of a big book or other enlarged text while directed and supported by an educator or other accomplished reader. Children observe a proficient reader reading the text with fluency and expression. The text must be large enough for all the children to see clearly so they share in the reading of the text. The reading process and reading strategies that readers use are revealed through shared reading.

Children who partake in shared reading learn critical concepts of how print works. They get the feel of learning and begin to perceive themselves as readers. Shared reading has many benefits; it

- allows children to enjoy materials that they may not be able to read on their own;
- ensures that all children feel successful by providing support to the entire group;
- allows children to act as though they are reading;
- helps novice readers learn about the relationship between oral language and printed language;
- assists children in learning where to look and/or how to focus their attention;
- supports children as they gain awareness of symbols and print conventions while they construct meaning from the text read;
- assists children in making connections between background knowledge and new information;
- focuses on and helps develop concepts about print and phonemic connections;
- helps teach frequently used words;
- encourages prediction in reading; and
- helps children develop a sense of story and increases their comprehension.

The shared reading experience also provides the opportunity for educators to share different types of books with children and familiarize them with some of their text features. Resources generally used for shared reading include fiction, poetry, and nonfiction books.

In the past, traditional shared reading used paper-based materials. Enlarged books, frequently in the form of big books, were the primary source of children's reading material. More recently, the materials have also incorporated posters, class-made books and information, and communication technology books. A number of electronic resources have been developed. One such resource online is Mimic Books. This resource has been specifically designed to be used on interactive whiteboards for shared reading lessons. The benefit of this resource is that it replicates the look and appearance of a real big book, but on the interactive whiteboard it is clearly visible to children.

A shared reading session may be directed in many ways, depending on the needs of the children and the teaching objectives determined by the educator. The educator typically selects books at the child's appropriate reading level. A shared reading typically starts with an educator reading a big book, making certain that everyone notices the book. He or she introduces the story, talking about the cover and title page, therefore engaging children in what they see in the cover picture and what they think it tells them about the story about to be read. During the introduction, an educator identifies specific character actions or events and asks probing questions to engage children in thinking about the pictures and story but does not tell the story.

As educators share the enlarged text with a group of children, they create instructional conversations that guide the children to apply their knowledge and strategies to the reading situation. One of the key aims of shared reading is to help children develop a variety of useful strategies for reading and comprehending books. Strategies are taught to help children with contextual word recognition and comprehension. Sessions must be planned in a progression, and it is important for educators to distinguish the purpose and learning aim of each session. In many cases, the educator and the children compile an assortment of books for shared reading.

The educator will expect increased participation from children whenever a familiar book is used for reading. Early learners generally have an increased interest in recognizable stories, songs, and rhymes. Moreover, if the stories have a predictable scheme, children are likely to participate early on in shared reading. As children develop, however, they must share more, have a better awareness of how stories are structured, and develop pleasure in an ever-increasing variety of books.

Educators need to be mindful that early readers do not become baffled by using shared reading to teach word recognition and phonics in combination with comprehension in the same session. At the conclusion of a session, educators must make copies of the book available to any child who desires to read it independently or with a peer, which allows children to examine the book better.

Shared reading sessions present several opportunities for children to hone their reading ability. In addition, they provide children with an opportunity to do the following:

- Concentrate on the use of their deciphering skills conducted in planned sessions. Educators must take into account each child's stage of phonics knowledge and skills.
- Develop phonological awareness by means of small-group teaching.
- Improve their vocabulary and experience the difference between written and spoken word within a wide assortment of books.
- Share and get pleasure from a variety of books and communicate their thoughts, ideas, and feelings. As a result, relationships with educators, parents, caregivers, and peers are developed.
- Increase comprehension of words read to them, therefore enhancing their comprehension skills.
- Recognize early any particular reading struggles.

Shared reading boosts reading as a shared effort within the classroom. Also, it allows children to support each other's efforts in the classroom throughout the reading experience. Indeed, it increases the chances of helping all peers, particularly the less-confident readers, which enables them to have a more successful reading experience. The National Reading Panel recommends that all children be exposed to and actively engaged in shared-book reading, which will stimulate verbal interactions.

Educators need to talk to parents and caregivers to build on and reinforce what they are teaching in the classroom so that children continue to learn at home. They must be trained and provided with instruction and materials to conduct shared reading with their children at home.

GUIDED READING

Guided reading is a teaching strategy that is conducted with a small number of children and focuses more on the individual reading needs of each child. It is designed to help individual children learn how to process a selection of progressively challenging texts with understanding and fluency. Guided reading has many of the same components as shared reading.

Throughout guided reading, the educator selects and introduces the texts to children, familiarizes children with the story ideas, connects the text to children's experiences, sometimes supports them while reading the text, engages the readers in discussion, and performs a mini-lesson after the reading. The lesson may include work with words based on the explicit needs of the small group. During a guided reading session, educators must work with children at the children's instructional level to guide them in using context, visual, and structural cues within stories to generate meaning. Using instructional level texts that gradually increase in difficulty, children apply strategies in context and become more successful. Instructional level is defined as a level where each child comprehends a minimum of 70 percent of the ideas and is 90 to 95 percent accurate with related word recognition.

The methods used in guided reading help children make sense of what they read, at first with help and later on their own. The educator provides support for small groups of readers as they learn to use several reading strategies. Guided reading traditionally has been associated with the primary grades. It makes best use of children's growth by enabling them to practice effective reading strategies on texts at or near their instructional level. Once supports and challenges of each text are evaluated, the educator provides sufficient guidance to help the children participate in reading problem-solving, balanced with a successful reading experience. Guided reading has the following six characteristics:

1. Children must be assigned to small groups of about four to six children each.
2. Guided reading lessons are to be about fifteen to twenty minutes long.
3. Educators must select reading material at the appropriate level for each child within the group to create success.
4. Educators must institute a purpose for reading that will provide the children with the accompanying information essential for the text.
5. Children read the selection individually. Children usually have the ability to read and comprehend most of the text. If a match for the age and reading level of the group is selected, they may encounter some unfamiliar words; nevertheless, children have the ability to problem-solve several of these unfamiliar words using a variety of strategies. The successful use of these strategies enables children to build self-confidence and proficiency as readers.
6. Educators must offer guidance to children based on observations when the children are reading the text. Further, educators need to use probing questions to make certain the children understand the text and then must praise their efforts. Likewise, educators must provide reminders and encouraging attempts at reading-strategy application.

It is vital to select texts for guided reading groups that match the needs of the children. Children who are provided suitable books have the ability to read with about 90 percent accuracy. As a result, they take pleasure in the story, because a reduced challenge will result in less interference with comprehension. Children will learn to focus on the meaning of the story and to apply various reading strategies to problem-solve when they do come across stumbling blocks in their knowledge.

Children who learn various reading strategies retain the essential skills and awareness to read more challenging texts. An educator who is aware of each child's abilities and needs as a reader must select books that have suitable supports and challenges for the children at each stage of their development. Educators must take time to acquaint themselves with the books in their classroom or school library. Additionally, they must organize books by levels or stages, so they easily reach for an appropriate book for a particular child.

Because independent reading is the goal, guided reading provides the framework to ensure that children are able to apply strategies to decipher sense from print. Although educators are the professionals at guided reading, they need to collaborate with parents and caregivers to make guided reading a successful strategy. Educators need to share with parents and caregivers some of the strategies they use at school with their children. For example, parents and caregivers must be informed that when their child is reading at home, even if the child is struggling, they must refrain from giving the answers. As an alternative to providing children with answers, parents and caregivers must be guided to ask probing questions to help their child accomplish the task successfully. Further, parents and caregivers must be instructed to ask questions pertaining to the word with which the child is having difficulty, such as, if the word follows a rule the child learned in class, or if it resembles a similar word the child knows. Similarly, if the child knows any part of the word, adults must ask the child the beginning, middle, or ending sounds.

Educators must urge parents and caregivers to provide their children with a pleasing, relaxed, and supportive reading experience. Most important is that children be offered consistent, routine reading experiences conducted regularly. Such experiences have a significant effect on a child's reading achievement.

INDEPENDENT READING

Independent reading is the reading children choose to undertake on their own or with companions. It is a strategy that must be used at every juncture of a child's reading development. Also called voluntary reading, leisure reading, or recreational reading, independent reading is not assigned or assessed, and it involves the child's personal choice of material. Independent reading is primarily conducted for information or for pleasure.

Independent reading must last about seven to fifteen minutes daily, with no disturbances. Children must be expected to select their books and read them without changing throughout the reading period and remain in a well-lit and accessible area of the classroom or home environment. The reading of meaningful connected text results in improved reading skills. Despite that fact, many children do not elect to read regularly or in great quantities. Only a few early learners choose to look at books during free-choice time at school, because many of them prefer to do other activities besides reading. Research indicates that children devote less than 2 percent of their free time to reading (Anderson et al., 1988).

Independent reading does three things:

1. Increases vocabulary. Evidence reveals that independent reading is perhaps the chief foundation of vocabulary expansion beyond the beginning stages of learning to read.
2. Builds fluency. Unless children accurately and easily manage the word-identification demands of reading, they will have difficulty with comprehension and reading success. In addition, a child's reading performance is increased if the child reads substantial quantities of text.
3. Builds background knowledge. Children's reading ability is influenced by the quantity of related information they have pertaining to the subject they are reading. By reading extensively, children are exposed to various subjects and information they can use for future reading.

During independent reading, educators become onlookers, acknowledging and responding to children's reading. Educators' central role is to select and collect appropriate books. They must provide materials that children read independently at the child's independent reading levels. This selection of books includes books that have been used in shared and guided reading, plus a large selection of other books.

Classroom and school libraries must provide children with high-quality books the children select independently. Unfortunately, this situation is not usually the case for schools in impoverished areas. In such circumstances, educators must build libraries from contributions and also urge parents and caregivers to take their children to a public library. Children read more books when they have more books available to them; and when they have a personal library, they read even more. It is essential for parents and caregivers to take their children to libraries and also purchase books for them, if affordable. Efforts must be made to find ways to send books to the homes of all children, especially to the homes of the children who are impoverished.

Educators must share with parents and caregivers, especially families of impoverished children, that Reading Is Fundamental (RIF) is an organization that provides children from birth to age eight and their families with new, free books to choose from and make their own. RIF, founded in 1966, is the largest and oldest nonprofit literacy organization in the United States. RIF trusts that it can inspire children to be lifelong readers through the power of choice. Its vision is a literate America in which all children have access to books and discover the joys and value of reading. Research indicates that through community volunteers in every state and U.S. territory, RIF provides 4.5 million children with 16 million new, free books and literacy resources each year. RIF's accomplishments are due in part to financial assistance by the U.S. Department of Education, corporations, foundations, community organizations, and thousands of individuals (Reading is Fundamental, 2009).

Educators must urge parents and caregivers to make sure their children continue reading at home. The amount of reading done out of school is consistently related to gains in reading success, yet most children devote very little time to reading at home. Roughly 50 percent of children read for only four minutes or less a day. Evidently this disparity is sufficient reason for parents and caregivers to increase the amount of reading their children accomplish at home (Anderson et al., 1988).

A 2010 scholastic study that resulted in "The Kids and Family Reading" report reveals that a child's reading frequency decreases after age eight. Furthermore, the study revealed that parents and caregivers have a direct influence on getting their children to read. When children start reading independently, parents and caregivers must become more, not less, involved. Besides, adults play a key role in helping their children learn to read. Parents and caregivers need to model routine reading at home with their children. A family that reads together grows in intellect as family members acquire new knowledge.

To become superb readers, children must read independently. It is helpful for children to read slightly easier books when they read independently, aiming for 90 percent comprehension and more than 95 percent word recognition. Children learn to read by having meaningful, realistic reading experiences and by getting support from more experienced individuals. For children to become proficient readers, they must have time to practice and apply their knowledge to reading.

Parents and caregivers, along with their child's educator, are the central trainers in developing a child's ability to read. These influential adults must be involved, by reading aloud to their children, knowing if their children are participating in shared or guided reading sessions, or simply knowing which books their children are reading independently at school.

To obtain help from parents and caregivers, educators must provide them with appropriate practice activities so they can continue to help their children at home. Similarly, parents and caregivers must support their children's efforts at school by communicating with their educators and inquiring about becoming parent volunteers, if needed, at school.

Educators, parents, and caregivers must support children in whatever strategy is viable for them to learn to read.

Equally important is to give children self-assurance, opportunity, and support while encouraging them to use their skills in a variety of situations and purposes. Undeniably, independent reading must be used at every step of a child's reading development. Educators working as a team with parents and caregivers must endeavor to move children from the earliest awareness of print to the reading-to-learn stage, where they will become independent, successful, and motivated readers.

IDENTIFYING AND NURTURING THE STRUGGLING READER

Teaching reading to early learners has always been an area of disagreement and debate. Children bring a wide range of ability levels to the classroom. The reasons that children struggle with learning to read are as varied as the children themselves. Consequently, no single approach to reading will meet the needs of all children. There is no simple answer to the question of what educators, parents, and caregivers must do when an early learner does not want to read. For certain, there will be challenges, and it will be vital that a collaborative force be formed among all participants in order to engage and inspire the struggling reader.

A child who has difficulty sounding out unknown words and who frequently misidentifies well-known words is considered a struggling reader. Such children read words with uncertainty and have numerous stops, starts, and mispronunciations. Furthermore, these children have poor comprehension. Some become struggling readers through lack of practice. As a result of this lack of involvement and exposure to reading methods, these children not only struggle but also may have a dislike for reading. For children who read less, vocabulary growth is limited and, consequently, their reading development is inhibited.

A large number of children from diverse backgrounds and social classes struggle to read. In general, a particular concern continues for struggling readers from low-income families. Struggling early learners are likely to need early interventions and ongoing support beyond the early years of schooling. For that reason, without interventions, struggling readers usually continue to have difficulty learning to read and fall further and further behind their peers. Struggling readers can reach average reading levels when they are given early, focused, and continuing support. Educational interventions that start early and continue for a longer time have larger and long-lasting benefits to children.

Small-group instruction is an important component for struggling readers. Small groups must consist of children with similar reading abilities. Within these groups, books and instructions are matched to the readers, so that the level of challenge is adequate but not overwhelming. Small groups permit educators to more easily sustain the focus and attention of children who may otherwise be disengaged. Additionally, such a setting allows educators to effortlessly monitor each child's reading behaviors and alter instructions and/or regroup the children, if and when necessary.

Small-group instruction, where instruction is individualized, allows children to work at suitably challenging levels with an educator's direct guidance. In addition to small-group instruction, there must be lessons in phonics and phonemic awareness, the application of deciphering strategies while reading related books, and the rereading of familiar, appropriate-level books.

In a 2009 study on "What Works for Struggling Children," researchers learned these three facts:

1. Regardless of the strategy used, programs that focus on phonics obtain much better results than those that do not.
2. Classroom instruction has a very positive effect on all children, including struggling readers. Educators must focus on their own skills, and through professional development, learn helpful classroom instruction that benefits every child, including struggling readers. Research-based instruction and skilled educators are key factors in teaching children to read in the early grades. Furthermore, trained educators are more effective than teaching assistants and volunteers. The latter two groups do improve reading performance, although not to the same extent as a trained educator; nevertheless, schools that have insufficient resources must use a blend of trained educators, teaching assistants, and volunteer tutors.
3. A well-designed tutoring program is a valuable strategy proven to be beneficial to struggling readers. Tutoring offers struggling children more targeted help. An effective program must embrace chances for phonemic awareness; phonics; comprehension; oral spelling and sounding of words; sight-word vocabulary development; and connections between reading, writing, and oral communication. In

many cases, tutoring is a paid service and obtainable based on parents' and caregivers' willingness or ability to pay for the services. In some cases, however, free tutoring is provided to parents and caregivers for their children, based on their inability to pay for services.

EDUCATORS SEEKING HELP FOR THE STRUGGLING READER

Educators must use some of the following activities to help struggling readers in their classroom:

- Familiarize themselves with the children and their parents and caregivers
- Encourage continued assistance at home
- Make use of specialists' resources within the school
- Search for professional development tools that help children incorporate the five components—phonemic awareness, phonics, vocabulary development, reading fluency, and reading comprehension—into their daily instruction
- Provide the parents and caregivers of children with school-based and outside resources for any available in-school tutoring programs or private tutoring
- Stay well versed in current information in the field of reading

Struggling readers benefit from effective collaborations connecting home and school. Educators must offer guidance to parents and caregivers to help them assist their children at home. Conversely, parents and caregivers must offer guidance to educators to help educators stimulate children at school. Educators must not assume parents and caregivers know how to help their children who are struggling. It is important to provide influencers with assistance in order for them to gain confidence in their ability to support their children at home.

Children need adults in their lives to direct and support them. Supportive home environments nurture motivation for reading, which leads to further voluntary reading and improved reading success. Many collaborative involvements linking home and school have increased the reading motivation of struggling readers as they improved their comprehension. Five types of collaborative involvements linking home and school are as follows:

1. Communicating by developing effective home-school communication
2. Volunteering by creating ways that parents and caregivers can become involved in activities at school

3. Learning at home by supporting learning activities in the home that reinforce children's activities in school
4. Decision making by including families as decision makers through the school site, such as councils and committees
5. Collaborating with the community by matching community services with family needs.

PARENTS AND CAREGIVERS SEEKING HELP FOR THE STRUGGLING READER

Parents and caregivers can launch a legacy by helping their children develop the gift of reading that will inspire their children and stay with them for the rest of their lives. Adults are not only critical role models for their children, but also their children's most important educators. If parents and caregivers recognize that their children are struggling with reading, they must trust their instinct and seek an evaluation. As the greatest influencers for their children, parents and caregivers need to make inquiries of their child's educators whenever they are unsure of how to help their children. To make sure their children have the best opportunity to become successful readers, parents and caregivers need to do the following:

- Learn if their child desires additional help
- Seek guidance from their child's educator
- Enlighten themselves about available alternatives
- Request an evaluation for their child, either school-based or from an outside source
- Most importantly, support their child at home

POINTS TO REMEMBER

A balanced teaching strategy is based on the concept that as children gain knowledge in learning to read, they will be supported at school and home. Ultimately, such support enables children to progressively accumulate sufficient knowledge and skills to function independently.

Balanced teaching strategies also integrate all reading approaches. Children who are exposed to multiple approaches tend to become superb readers. A good balance combines the teaching of phonics and whole language.

The whole-language method allows children to identify numerous words as effortlessly as they can various letters. Whole language provides children with a complete word in order to focus on meaning. Alternatively, phonics provides them with words letter by letter. Research has shown that highly literate readers always use phonics to decipher new words. Today, most educators in the United States combine phonics with some elements of whole language to teach children to read.

Equally important are reading aloud to children, shared reading, guided reading with small groups, and independent reading.

Reading aloud models fluent reading, promotes enjoyment and appreciation of children's literature, develops vocabulary knowledge, stimulates and motivates independent reading, and, most importantly, develops bonds. Shared reading is an interactive reading experience that occurs when children join or share the reading of a big book or other enlarged text while directed and supported by an educator or other skilled reader. Guided reading is a teaching strategy that is conducted with a small number of children and focuses more on the individual reading needs of each child. Guided reading helps children learn how to process a selection of progressively challenging texts with understanding and fluency. Independent reading is the reading children choose to do on their own or with companions. It is an approach that must be used at every stage of a child's reading development.

Many children struggle with learning to read; however, a child who has difficulty sounding out unknown words and who frequently misidentifies well-known words is considered a struggling reader. Reading failure creates long-term negative effects for children, such as losing their self-confidence and the motivation to learn. On a positive note, struggling readers can reach average reading levels when they are given early, focused, and ongoing support.

3

📖

Engaging Readers through Books and Technology

Technology surrounds children at home, schools, and in their communities. It not only changes society, but it is also an integral part of children's lives. Children now live in a fast-changing, technology-driven world; and technology plays an important role in their education, directly and indirectly affecting their daily lives.

Technological advances pushed the United States into a digital upheaval that transformed our society. For children to become successful adults, educators, parents, and caregivers must provide children with technological knowledge and experiences in their early years. Regardless of a child's socioeconomic level, race, ethnic background, or disability, each absolutely must have access to technology.

Although children need to know how to read books and write with pen and paper, they must also learn how to navigate and master technology. Technology provides numerous media devices to bring information to children, with constant innovation and change. Primarily, computer technology brings change in the way educators teach and deliver vast resources for parents and caregivers to assist their children.

Since the early 1980s, the use of technology—in particular, computers—has continued to rise in programs for early learners. Personal computers emerged as consumer products near the end of the 1970s and were named *Time* magazine's "person of the year" in 1982. People with children hastily embraced personal computers. Likewise, many homes quickly connected to the Internet when it became accessible to the general public in the early 1990s.

Today, children all over the world use computers and Internet technology. Within the United States, the National Center for Education

Statistics indicates that virtually every school with access to computers has 99 percent Internet access. The National Education Technology Plan promotes universal access to technology for all children. The technology requirements of the No Child Left Behind Act include resources and best practices on technology literacy and effective teaching using technology. Lawmakers who drafted the NCLB want all children to be exposed to and to be capable of using computers and the Internet at an early age. In addition, the NCLB demands that all children must be technologically literate by the end of the eighth grade.

This chapter covers using the library, technology and learning with computers, technology and the building blocks for teaching early learners to read, technology and early learners' motivation, and lesson plans incorporating reading and technology.

USING THE LIBRARY

Getting access to books is one of the most important factors affecting a child's reading ability. Books are silent on the shelf until readers give them voice. Once that voice is found, worlds of value, imagination, and reason are opened.

Libraries offer children a wealth of knowledge through access to books, compact discs, audiocassettes, videos, computers, and many more resources. Libraries furnish information about culture, society, economy, and history. They provide a wide access to high-quality books on various topics in many fields and from a variety of viewpoints, all of which help learners achieve good reading skills. Through libraries, children have access to a wide variety of reading materials and other activities, such as arts and crafts, songs, drama, storytelling, and puppet shows. Libraries' learning facilities and materials have stimulated public discussion through the resources in their collections.

Certainly the great quantities of print and meaningful language opportunities libraries hold offer children the essentials for reading achievement. Children who are exposed to libraries in their early years demonstrate a higher level of pre-reading skills than those who are not exposed to libraries. Indeed, libraries play an important role in the development of children's reading skills in our nation.

Parents in low- and middle-class families differ widely in the skills and resources they have for advancing their children's reading skills outside of school. Sometimes children from these types of households lack access to books and other reading material in their daily lives. Libraries are valuable sources for these families, because libraries furnish children of all backgrounds access to high-quality reading materials, enriching their experiences and allowing them the opportunity to succeed. Librarians work to ensure that without regard to children's socioeconomic status, all children can reach their full potential as readers.

Many libraries offer summer reading programs to attract children. In the summertime, children's reading skills often decline, because children are away from the classroom and not participating in formal literacy programs. Educators must endeavor to raise parents and caregivers' awareness of the importance of supporting their children's reading development during the summertime by participating in summer reading programs.

Also, educators must provide influencers with recommendations, such as a list of books, a journal, or logbook for their children to record what they have read during the summer. Children's continual reading in the summertime allows educators and children to begin afresh, instead of starting over when the next school year begins. Children who partake in these programs generally improve their reading levels before they go into the next grade, particularly because these programs keep children engaged in reading and learning.

Many libraries also offer story times as an effective way of exposing early learners to the library and boosting their love of reading. Educators, parents, and caregivers need to take children to the library for story time. In many libraries, a library staff member is available during story time to share specific ways in which educators, parents, and caregivers can produce a more valuable reading experience for their children.

Library programs offer priceless opportunities for children to spend time with books. Library programs are excellent steps toward the development of a child's reading skills. Simply visiting the library encourages children to spend more time in a learning-enriched atmosphere. Children who participate in summer reading programs benefit from the programs' many literacy-related activities. In addition to reading books, these children can participate in story times, arts and crafts, and special events designed to extend literacy experiences while reading books. Likewise, time at a library presents a child the opportunity to look around and check out books and other materials that interest them.

Educators must encourage parents and caregivers to create a library at home for their children, which allows children to have access to books at all times. Likewise, educators need to construct their own libraries for children within their classrooms to encourage children to read more. Children commonly read books in their classroom, even if a school library is nearby. Although true, educators must arrange for children to visit their school library weekly. A school library is able to make available a greater variety of materials than a classroom library.

Many educators increase the accessibility of their classroom materials by using their own resources. In some schools, educators donate books from their personal collections to a central storage location for sharing. Books are also collected through book clubs, school book fairs, or contributions from parents, businesses, or organizations. In addition, collections can be shared among classes. Some public libraries make available many books at a time for educators; nevertheless, book availability must be a school-wide combined effort among educators, administrators, parents, and caregivers.

Research reveals that 97 percent of Americans agree that school library programs are an essential part of the education experience, because they provide resources to children and educators. Another 96 percent agree that school libraries are important because they give every child the opportunity to learn to read (American Library Association, 2009).

With encouragement and help from educators, parents, and caregivers, children can even establish a small library in their own bedroom. If not a bedroom, a special place should be selected at home where early learners store their own books. Provide adequate shelving space for the early learners to sort and organize their books. Caution must be taken not to place library books with a child's own books. Some early learners may require assistance to sort and organize their books. A home library indicates to children that books are important and enjoyable and encourages them to read more.

Educators, parents, and caregivers must spend time with children selecting books at the library to take home and put in a child's special place for reading. Computers have also made it easier for parents and caregivers to sit with their children and reserve books online that they can get at the library when available for pickup. Surely parents and caregivers must help their child select books or take a few suggested titles they will read together; however, children must be allowed to make their own selections. Giving children the opportunity to choose their own books lets them be active participants in their own reading routine, which increases the likelihood of their reading.

Books with repetition, predictability, and great illustrations are the best for the earliest learners' reading success. Most important is for all concerned adults to become actively involved with their child's reading progress. To boost reading at home, educators must encourage parents and caregivers to read library books with their child, which gives early readers a model to go by. Regular trips to the library are vital to a child's reading success.

Today, public libraries are challenged to do more with less money, less staff, and less time. Educators, parents, and caregivers need to let their communities know the importance of their public library and rally to increase public funds to ensure that the library has the necessary resources to be current. Support is vital for the continual success of public libraries.

Studies confirm that reading achievement is related to book access. In one study, researchers found that when elementary school children who had little exposure to books were taken to a library, it made a huge difference in their reading and interest in reading. Research indicates that 217 million Americans agree or strongly agree that the public library improves the quality of life in their community. More than 222 million Americans also agree or strongly agree that libraries provide free access to materials and resources, and the public library plays a vital role that permits all children to succeed (American Library Association, 2009).

Continual parental involvement in children's early years is vital to help them become successful readers. For that reason, educators must stress to parents and caregivers the importance of taking their children to the public library and obtaining a library card. Again, educators must encourage subsequent and regular visits to check out books. Likewise, collaboration among educators, librarians, media specialists, parents, and caregivers contributes to early learners' preparation for success at reading, because all participants strengthen each other's efforts.

TECHNOLOGY AND LEARNING WITH COMPUTERS

The appeal of computers has become important to early learners. Consequently, there has been a fundamental shift in what it means "to read." In 1971, Michael S. Hart created the first electronic book (e-book) by typing the United States Declaration of Independence into a computer.

An e-book, also called a digital book, is a book-length publication in digital form that consists of text, images, or both, and it is produced, published, and read on computers or other electronic devices. The *Oxford Dictionary of English* defines the e-book as an electronic version of a printed book, but e-books exist without any printed equivalent. E-books are often read on dedicated e-book readers, such as the Amazon Kindle, the Nook, the iPad, or other tablet computers. Personal computers and some mobile phones are also used to read e-books.

On May 19, 2011, *Forbes* magazine reported that Amazon.com, the world's largest Internet retailer and bookseller, had announced that its sale of e-books had surpassed its sale of printed books. This milestone occurred four years after Amazon.com released the Kindle electronic reader (e-reader) in November 2007. This news indicates that over the Internet, at least, e-books are being purchased more often than print books.

The e-book represents the combination of the advantages of the printed book with the capabilities of the computer. Moreover, e-books have the capability of adding more to text and picture in terms of animation, sounds, and narration. These additions are attractive to early learners.

E-books encourage reading, in particular by learners who are reluctant readers. Consequently, e-books undoubtedly will have an influence on early learners' future reading methods and offer hope for them to have a more contemporary, hands-on method of gaining access to information.

Today's technologically advanced world needs skills that are greater than those required of previous generations. Consequently, it is imperative that educators, parents, and caregivers explore many technologies, such as e-books or tablet computers, to engage early learners in reading and using their imagination. These influencers must all partner to prepare children for a world filled with technology and a diversity of reading methods.

Technology offers unique intellectual experiences and opportunities for early learners. Computers stimulate them, and the sounds and graphics gain their attention. Developmentally appropriate software engages early learners in creative play, mastery learning, problem solving, and conversation. Furthermore, early learners can use computers to create art, make music, tell and record stories, hear their stories read back to them, and play educational games that are able to connect with off-screen learning and play.

Although computers cannot replace all reading activities for early learners, they can support these activities. As early learners develop more skills to read on their own, they are not limited to understanding only icons and pictures on the computer screen. More opportunities for independent use become available with increasing reading skills.

Computer reading allows early learners to do the following:

- Hear stories, read along, sing along, and read individually
- Play with objects and characters on the screens that teach the alphabet, simple words, rhyming words, and other skills important to learning to read
- Command the computer by voice, record themselves reading, and play back the recording, so that they hear themselves
- Write simple sentences and make up stories
- Add pictures and characters to their stories and have them read back, make and print their own books, and create slide shows

Early learners can be introduced to technology beginning at age three or four. Researchers found that three- and four-year-olds who use computers have greater developmental achievements, in contrast to peers who do not have computer experience. Additionally, research indicates that computers boost children's development of positive attitudes toward learning and help them advance their spoken communication. Furthermore, the role that technology plays in the home in reading and achievement for kindergartners and first graders shows that children's access to and use of technology influences their future reading capabilities. It is therefore essential for educators to team up with parents and caregivers to help them educate early learners on how to use computers and the Internet.

Educators must develop careful plans and share them with parents and caregivers for their early learners to use the computer. These plans must allow children to discover new opportunities. An effective way to introduce early learners to technology is to show them online stories, because high-quality online stories allow for interactivity and engage children in a different form of learning. Unlike paper books, online activities give children access to dynamic texts with videos, audio, and links to other sites.

Many online websites provide popular stories that include animation, oral narration, or word pronunciation on demand. These sites can be interactive and match a child's learning style, such as visual, hands-on, and auditory. Some sites offer context clues and organizing structures, such as illustrations and clickable definitions of unfamiliar terms that help early learners develop stronger comprehension skills. In addition, some websites make children predict what they will read next, which allows children to make more forward inferences than they may make in paper books. Most important, when children have the choice to select their own online reading stories, they take ownership of their reading.

Reading online allows children to become dependent on their critical thinking skills to discover information. An increasing number of online resources are available for classroom use. There are many benefits in the use of e-books available through well-known publishers, such as Scholastic. The following are other websites for building a strong reading foundation that educators can share with parents and caregivers:

- KidSpace@the Internet (http://www.ipl.org/div/kidspace/browse/rzn2000) offers numerous interactive picture book stories for children to read online and links to other interesting websites with interactive K-3-appropriate stories.
- The International Children's Digital Library (http://www.icdlbooks.org) provides a wealth of colorfully illustrated books that include interesting plots. The website does not charge a fee, and books from around the world are presented in several languages.
- StoryLine Online (http://www.storylineonline.net) is a list of read-aloud books available on the Internet. This website offers children's books read aloud by well-known movie and television actors from the Screen Actors Guild Foundation. Extra activities are contained within each book that asks children to draw inferences and retell the story. The website also has a telephone service that allows children to call in and listen to an actor read a book.

Educators must stress to parents and caregivers the issues involved with children's use of technology and inform parents and caregivers of the resources available to guide their children through this dynamic environment. Likewise, educators must direct parents and caregivers to the many excellent websites that provide guidelines for sensible Internet use and inform them of the links to child-appropriate websites and instructional and educational sites. See appendix F for an added list of educational literacy websites.

Early learners with special educational needs and those who learn English as a second language also benefit from computer technology. Computers, along with other assistive devices, have a transformational effect on these early learners. For instance, technology allows children to progress at their own pace, according to their learning styles. Moreover, children have a private place for practice, while learning without fear of public failure. This advantage is especially helpful during their early years, when they are expected to attain an acceptable level of mastery.

Computers are becoming a vital tool in life, and learning to use them is crucial to function in today's society. Educators must provide parents and caregivers with support to ensure early learners' success with using technology. Make certain children become familiar with the computer and the activities in children's software programs. Each child needs to know the basics of the computer and how it works. Children who lack experience or who are reluctant to learn about the computer must be given focused assistance to become more at ease with technology. Emphasis must be placed on how to use programs in intended ways, to provide the appropriate level of challenge for every early learner.

To foster collaboration, educators need to invite parents and caregivers into the classroom as volunteers during computer hours. Educators must introduce the reading programs they use and explain to parents and caregivers the programs' benefits. Sadly, educational technology has the potential to exclude children who do not have access to it and who are not able to use it; and, regrettably, these children are typically in financially disadvantaged situations. For families of children who do not have computers at home, educators must inform parents and caregivers of local places with computer access, such as the public library or community centers.

Educators must also encourage parents and caregivers who are hesitant to use the computer to keep a printed copy of software program guides near the computer, use video tutorials, explore free online tutorials, and/or request assistance from a friend or teenager who is familiar with the computer. In addition, parents and caregivers need to be encouraged to learn more through technology workshops in their community, such as their local library or adult learning center. These programs increase parents' and caregivers' own knowledge and comfort with computers, therefore giving them the ability to advance their children's reading efforts. Early learners' reading efforts are enhanced when parents are purposely engaged in school and home activities that support not only their children's learning, but also their own learning.

Technology is changing the world and the United States educational system. It is a tool that provides another way for early learners to make sense of their world. Today many resources are available to help early learners excel at reading. Computers add to the tools available for early learners to explore, create, and communicate. Educators, parents, and caregivers must, however, use good judgment in evaluating and using technology appropriately. Choosing appropriate software for early learners is similar to choosing appropriate books at school or home.

The amazing, ever-changing technological world seems overwhelming at times, but technology must be part of an early learner's reading curriculum, and it definitely continues to be an asset to children's quest of information. Further, technology boosts their interest in reading. Concerned individuals must rise to the challenge of acquiring available resources. Educators must be mindful of new technological developments, for example, through professional development. Educators are urged to share their findings with parents and caregivers to provide opportunities for children to develop their proficiencies in school.

Technology continues to infuse every aspect of society. Educators have a central role to provide children with the opportunity to use technology in meaningful and authentic tasks. Technology-rich classrooms free educators from the constraints of textbooks and give them the chance to complete other tasks. Moreover, technology gives children access to the most up-to-date information, unavailable in traditional textbooks. It offers new opportunities that stimulate lines of inquiry previously unimagined in early learners.

Technology must be a part of early learners' reading curriculum; and educators, parents, and caregivers must have access to technology to help early learners learn to read. Early experiences with the Internet, computers, and other technologies in school and at home are crucial for the development of the knowledge and skills early learners need for future literacy and twenty-first-century skills.

TECHNOLOGY AND THE BUILDING BLOCKS
FOR TEACHING EARLY LEARNERS TO READ

A central concern of today's educators, parents, and caregivers is how technology affects children's academic achievement. A growing concern in our society is to develop approaches to motivate the growing number of children who have not been successful in learning how to read. Research indicates that computer-assisted instruction provides an effective tool to help struggling readers.

Combining the five research-based reading components issued by the National Reading Panel with the effective use of technology offers children opportunities to achieve reading success. The five research-based components of effective reading instruction as it relates to technology for teaching early learners to read are as follows:

1. *Phonemic awareness.* Computers present a variety of phonemic awareness practice activities and provide feedback and reports to educators, parents, and caregivers about their children's progress. Many software programs for early learners incorporate matching activities, in which children are directed to match a sound with pictures of objects that start with that sound, a sequence of sounds with the word they form when blended together, or pictures of objects with names that start with the same sound or rhyme. In these types of activities, many of the capabilities of computers do the following:

   a. Provide tasks that segment and blend words into sounds
   b. Provide immediate feedback to let children know if their answers are correct and, if not, opportunities for corrections
   c. Individualize problems to focus on the phonemes that children have not yet mastered
   d. Repeat activities and alter the speed of speech to meet individual needs
   e. Provide activities that ask children to match sounds and letters
   f. Offer activities designed for two or three children to work together
   g. Provide game contexts, attractive visual presentations, and speeches that capture attention and motivate children to engage
   h. Provide reports for educators on a child's progress and areas where a child needs additional help
   i. Engage children in productive self-directed work on phonemic awareness, which enables educators to have more time to meet the individual needs of each child

2. *Phonics.* Many of the capabilities of computers for phonics instruction overlap those already described for phonemic awareness instruction. In fact, many of the software applications that support phonics development also make use of additional support to enable phonics practice to be combined with reading meaningful text and with children's writing. Potential uses of technology to enhance phonics instruction include the ability to do the following:

a. Provide tasks that involve having children match sounds and letters, spoken and written words. In some cases, it simply involves adding letters and a written-word component to phonemic awareness activities.
b. Provide immediate feedback to let children know whether their answers are correct, give children hints or additional chances, and provide correct answers
c. Individualize problem sets and present stories to focus on the letter-sound correspondence and words that a child has not yet mastered
d. Provide as many repetitions as necessary and alter the speed of speech to meet a child's individual needs
e. Provide game contexts, attractive visual presentations, and speeches that capture attention and motivate children to engage
f. Provide reports for educators on a child's progress and areas where a child requires additional help. Also it provides texts for children to read that support phonic skills; for example, software that enables a child to click on any word and hear the individual sounds of the word or the whole spoken word.
g. Engage children in productive self-directed work on phonics while an educator helps other children, which allows educators more time to meet the individual needs of each child.

3. *Vocabulary development.* The teaching recommendations suggest several ways in which technology supports vocabulary development in children, including the ability to do the following:

a. Make available online interactive vocabulary lessons with features that engage children, offer feedback, individualize instruction, and keep records for educators
b. Provide online dictionaries, thesauri, and encyclopedias, with speech capabilities in order to give children access to tools to use with their word-learning strategies
c. Furnish online texts with hyperlinks that give children definitions of words and further information about key ideas in the text
d. Give children additional opportunities to extend their vocabularies by increasing the amount of reading they do through the use of online materials and exchanges. Examples of such opportunities include websites, discussions, and other technology-enabled uses of text.

4. *Reading fluency.* E-books present traditional picture-book text and images in an alternative on-screen format. The simplest e-books simply transfer the story from paper to the screen, which allows

children to listen as a program reads the story aloud. Some e-books may also highlight each word as the child progresses through the book. More complex e-books create more manageable stories that allow children to manipulate the text and introduce features not found in traditional books. E-books with features designed specifically to support children learning to read fluently provide multiple supports for fluency instruction, including the ability to do the following:

a. Provide a model of fluent oral reading
b. Furnish on-demand or automated help in decoding individual words, so problems with a few words do not disrupt the child's reading
c. Supply visual highlighting of phrases to guide a child in learning to read with expression
d. Allow early readers to encounter varied and challenging texts with additional support for pronunciation and meaning, which enables them to read independently with more success and gain added experience with text
e. Provide speech recognition tools so that children get immediate help while reading aloud
f. Offer recording and study tools for educators to evaluate a child's levels of fluency and make instructional decisions.

5. *Reading comprehension.* Technology provides direct instruction in comprehension strategies through the ability to do the following:

a. Provide hypertext and hypermedia that include the supporting of children's text comprehension to improve their knowledge; for example, clarifications, summaries, concept maps, and key questions related to specific parts of a text. Hypertext is text displayed on a computer with references to other text the reader is able to access immediately, usually by a mouse click or key-press sequence. Hypermedia is a computer-based information retrieval system that provides access to texts, audio and video recordings, photographs, and computer graphics related to the subject.
b. Furnish (inserted prompts that probe children to respond) to questions, add to graphic organizers, and summarize information.
c. Encourage active reading by having options to read words aloud, provide definitions, explain concepts in texts, and provide visual aids. These supports help children experience success in reading, provide learning opportunities within the context of meaningful texts, engage them in reading, and encourage the active use of comprehension strategies.

The five components and the technology teaching recommendations from the National Reading Panel must be incorporated as children learn to read. Children who cannot recognize or decipher written words are unable to read fluently or understand the meanings of words and are therefore limited in their text-comprehension abilities. Learning through technology and reading meaningful texts at appropriate levels of difficulty are ways for children to increase their vocabulary and practice their phonics skills. To build meaning from written texts, accomplished readers combine all the components of reading with their prior knowledge about what they are reading.

Today's children are born into a world of digital technology. The increased access to information through new technologies helps educators, parents, and caregivers assist children in achieving their full potential as enthusiastic readers. Computer and Internet technology engage early learners and teach them certain skills, competencies, and knowledge that contribute to reading success. As technologies become more advanced and innovative, educators, parents, and caregivers need to keep abreast, increase their knowledge, and put their energies into shaping content to make technology a positive force in the lives of children.

TECHNOLOGY AND EARLY LEARNERS' MOTIVATION

Technology has a profound effect on children's motivation to learn to read. Technological hardware and software promote early learners' engagement, motivation, and learning proficiencies. The National Reading Panel noted that although the cognitive aspects of reading, such as comprehension and decoding, are commonly recognized as vital components within the overall process of learning to read, motivation also is a critical factor in a child's reading success. Graphics, animation, and sound effects are constant eye-openers or ear catchers for early learners.

Research reveals that children who use hypermedia-based software to learn letter recognition were enthusiastic about using computers and became motivated to explore and learn from the software. Also, kindergarten and first-grade children who were presented with similar paper and electronic resources preferred to wait for an opportunity to use the electronic version, even if a print version was available.

Additional studies indicate that children's motivation to use the computer persists even after the computers become unavailable. Children also show enthusiasm for using reading software, even when they are unenthusiastic to work on reading concepts the software targeted. Other research indicates that some children respond to the computer software who would not respond to an educator's interventions. Third-grade children who worked on CD-ROM storybooks expressed that they like the pronunciation features and definitions.

Increased flexibility, support, responsiveness to children, and visual attractiveness of computer-presented hypertext and hypermedia are valuable tools to increase children's motivation to read. Research reveals that with the help of technology, many educators report noticeable increases in the number of hours children spend on recreational reading, the number of children who have library cards, and the number of children ordering summer book-club memberships. Likewise, parents and caregivers also report that their children are more excited about reading.

The review of the research on technology and teaching children to read leads to the conclusion that multimedia (media and content that use a combination of content forms, which includes a combination of text, audio, still images, animation, video, or interactivity content forms) digital technology, with capabilities such as hypertext, text-to-speech conversion, and speech recognition, has significant potential to motivate early learners' to read. This potential is significant for struggling readers, because the technology provides appropriate levels of activities, repetitive practice, individualized feedback, and detailed record keeping to inform instructional decisions. Technology helps educators, parents, and caregivers provide more of the individualized instruction that struggling readers need.

Opportunities to read arise from a large collection of resources in every format, from print to digital, whether at school, home, or the library. Early learners who have accessibility to these resources are in the best positions to increase their reading achievements. To advance the technological fluency of our nation's children, we need to start teaching technology in the learners' early years.

Technology is driving exceptional advances in both our society and our schools. Today, children are comfortable with technology and are not afraid to explore new software and tools. It is the responsibility of educators, parents, and caregivers to introduce children to technological opportunities and bridge the connection between what they do at school and at home, which will allow children to acquire the necessary skills for technological success. Children of the twenty-first century need to be technologically literate to grow and thrive in a global community that values technology literacy and innovation. It is the responsibility of all influencers to ensure that all early learners use the technology necessary to become skilled readers.

The following is a list of a few effective reading programs for children:

- Academy of Reading
- Breakthrough to Literacy
- Daisy Quest
- Fast for Word

- IBM Writing to Read
- Little Planet Literacy Series
- Project LISTEN
- SuccessMaker
- Tomorrow's Promise Reading
- Watch me! Read
- Waterford Early Reading Program
- Wiggle Works

LESSON PLANS INCORPORATING
READING AND TECHNOLOGY

Technology is now a part of the educational process and must be incorporated into educators' lesson plans for early learners. The goal is to promote and extend children's learning and increase their opportunity to be competitive in today's digital world. Technology also has the potential to connect children with reading and revitalize reading instructions to make them more relevant in the lives of children.

There are no federally sanctioned national standards for any academic area; curricula are developed at the state and local level. The school system and state and national curriculum frameworks and learning standards define—and, in some cases, mandate—what educators teach. Lesson planning must therefore be connected to local curriculum frameworks, which are aligned to state and national standards. Even so, no local curriculum or national standard outlines everything to be taught to children in the classroom. Educators must select what they teach children. The National Curriculum Standards for reading and educational computing and technology are the International Reading Association (IRA) and the International Society for Technology in Education (ISTE).

Technology provides several media devices to convey information to children, with continual innovation and change. Primarily, computer technology is used to help early learners develop proficiency in reading by constructing a global channel for children to communicate, investigate, and access information. Technology investments for children, who will be our future citizens, benefit communities and businesses and enhance economic vitality.

Economic research by Nobel Prize winners and Federal Reserve economists reveals that the return in public investments in high-quality childhood education is substantial. Consequently, children who are not introduced to technology at an early age fail to benefit from a valuable teaching tool that could have improved their academic success in later years. Tables 3.1 and 3.2 shows lesson plans that educators can use to incorporate reading and technology.

Table 3.1   State Web Page Lesson Plan

State Web Page Lesson Plan	
Objective:	Today the class is going to conduct a search on the Internet to find websites and analyze the content to make sure it is appropriate for providing information on Georgia's history.
Lesson Duration:	Four weeks
Required Resources:	➤ Internet Access—Netscape ➤ Computers
Instruction:	Educator Preparation ➤ Divide the study of Georgia into parts, such as geography of Georgia, early Georgia, and present Georgia. ➤ Divide children into groups. ➤ Prepare worksheets. Prerequisite Student Skills ➤ Children need to know keyboarding and be taught how to bookmark websites and navigate them. ➤ Some knowledge of using search engines is helpful. Activities/Procedures ➤ Children will research about five websites that have age-appropriate information about Georgia. ➤ Children will create questions. ➤ Each group will plan a Web page using the educator's worksheet. ➤ Each group of children will construct a section of the Web page. Sections will be organized and blended into one page. Assessment/Evaluation Children must ➤ Analyze and determine the value of accessed sites. ➤ Create five to ten multiple-choice questions appropriate to the study of Georgia. ➤ Research their questions for answers on the websites. ➤ Demonstrate their knowledge of Georgia's history. ➤ Demonstrate ability to use appropriate technology. ➤ Demonstrate ability to work in groups.
Follow-up:	Publicize the Georgia Web page and move on to the next topic in the curriculum.

Table 3.2 Culture Lesson Plan

Culture Lesson Plan	
Objective:	Today the class is going to conduct a search on the Internet to learn that all cultures have value.
Lesson Duration:	Two days
Required Resources:	➢ CultureGrams Kids Edition for the countries being researched ➢ CultureGrams Online Edition–Photo Gallery
Instruction:	➢ Assign each child to read a selected Kids Edition. CultureGrams report from one of the countries selected. Children must be instructed to pay particular attention to categories dealing with daily life in another country—for example, land and climate, games and sports, food, life as children, and transportation.
	➢ Have children browse through their assigned country's photo album from the CultureGrams Online Edition. Children must be instructed to pay particular attention to pictures that display people, activities, food, and living conditions.
	➢ Place children in groups according to country. Have them brainstorm points to incorporate in a written homework assignment in which they imagine what their life would have been like if they lived in their assigned country. Children can select to write about an ordinary day, a holiday, or a public event.
	➢ Children must be instructed that some of the information for their written assignment needs to be taken from the CultureGrams report and pictures.
	➢ On the second day, have children read their written assignments and discuss the similarities and differences they learned.
	Children must be encouraged to use their imaginations in deciding what life in the foreign country might be like.
Follow-up:	A written homework assignment Post children's assignment on a board outside the classroom.

Early learners need to read, select, and make use of related information from conducting their research using the computer. Educators must explain the following to children:

- Viewing websites allows them to conduct research and acquire information online.
- How best to research information online; for example, outlining specific steps to discern a goal, establishing necessary or missing information, and evaluating secondary sources.
- The necessity of selecting websites and computer activities that are at their appropriate reading levels.

POINTS TO REMEMBER

Today's children are bombarded by technology. Technology surrounds children in schools, in their homes, and in their communities. For children to become successful adults, it is vital for educators, parents, and caregivers to provide their children with technological knowledge and experiences in their early years. Although children need to know how to read books and write with pen and paper, it is crucial that they also learn how to navigate and master technology. The NCLB Act requires that all children be technologically literate by the end of the eighth grade.

Getting access to books is one of the most important factors affecting a child's reading abilities. Libraries offer children a wealth of knowledge, as well as access to books, compact discs of books, audiocassettes, videos, computers, and many more resources to support their learning. The library's great quantities of print and meaningful language opportunities give children the essentials for reading achievement. Many libraries offer summer reading programs and story times. Also, school and home libraries can be created. Collaboration among educators, librarians, media specialists, parents, and caregivers contributes to early learners' preparation for success at reading, because all participants strengthen each other's efforts.

There has been a fundamental shift in what it means "to read." The sales of e-books have surpassed the sale of paper books in some markets. As a result, e-books undoubtedly will have an influence on early learners' future reading. Educators, parents, and caregivers need to explore different technologies and engage early learners to use technology to read and use their imagination. Computers are exciting for early learners, because the sounds and graphics gain their attention; however, educators, parents, and caregivers must develop a careful plan for early learners to use the computer. They must be mindful of new technological developments and provide opportunities for children to develop their proficiencies at school and home.

Technology has a profound effect on children's motivation to learn to read. The National Reading Panel noted that although the cognitive aspects of reading, such as comprehension and decoding, are commonly recognized as vital components in the overall process of learning to read, motivation also is a critical factor in a child's reading success. This fact has also been reinforced by researchers. Undeniably, technology is a great tool to explore sensible approaches that meet the needs of children, educators, parents, and caregivers. Today's technologically driven world is full of exciting, innovative ways to teach early learners to read. Nevertheless, there needs to be a balance of traditional and emerging resources, tools, and approaches that are effective, efficient, and appealing to everyone.

4

📖

Learning to Read and Reading to Learn: Children's Literature

Children's literature generally consists of books intentionally written for children to read; however, the most comprehensive definition of children's literature relates to books that are actually selected and read by children. On the other hand, the most restrictive definition of children's literature cites books that various authorities determine are suitable for children, such as educators, reviewers, researchers, parents, caregivers, publishers, librarians, retailers, and various book-award committees.

Before the nineteenth century, only a few books were written specifically for children. In the twentieth century, technological advancements, such as the computer, paved the way for the creation of beautifully illustrated, well-bound books, thus transforming publishing. A wide exposure to children's literature at school and home stimulates children to learn to read effortlessly and achieve knowledge in a natural setting.

Children's literature is fundamental to teaching reading and is a rich source of vocabulary. Literature geared toward children engages and motivates them to read, provides them with a meaningful understanding of subject matter, and is a source from which they acquire information about their culture and that of their peers. Indeed, children's literature is a source through which early learners virtually enter the hearts, minds, lives, and spirits of others.

Piaget's theories of child development support the use of children's literature with early learners. According to Piaget, children between two and seven years of age fit into the preoperational period of development, when children express views but think intuitively rather than logically.

For example, research reveals that two- and three-year-old children believe that if lifeless objects move, they are alive. Similarly, Piaget found that early learners believed the moon followed them when they went for a walk at night, that dreams came through the window while they were asleep, and that anything that moved, including the waves and wind-blown curtains, was alive. Piaget describes this childhood trait at this phase as individual reasoning, which makes children enjoy magic tales without questioning the logic of a story.

The early years are the most sensitive period for early learners to experience children's literature. In these years, children have a great deal of imagination and creativity to interpret stories and relate them to their lives. Children must be provided with a rich assortment of children's books to exploit language in imaginative and meaningful ways. These books must, however, offer realistic and meaningful contexts for learning.

Passed down from generation to generation in children's literature is the language of story created by words. Early learners imagine themselves in the books they read, as they associate and relate to characters, places, and events. Children's literature reflects early learners' lives, as learners marvel at the lives in the story. Likewise, learners recognize themselves and the world. The events in the stories are ways in which learners explore the world.

Stories can be fiction or nonfiction; however, the most common methods of choosing children's literature are according to genre and reading level. A genre is a category of literature defined by shared characteristics, such as style, content, and theme. Within some genres, there are subgenres.

This chapter discusses the Newbery and Caldecott Medal books and other best children's books for early learners, as well as the following types of children's literature: picture books, easy reader books, chapter books, nonfiction books, fiction books, traditional literature books, biography books, and poetry books.

THE BEST CHILDREN'S BOOKS FOR EARLY LEARNERS

Numerous children's books are published annually. Educators must therefore narrow the field of potential books. By directing their attention to award-winning literature such as books that have won the Newbery and Caldecott Awards, they can narrow the field of potential books that might seem overwhelming. Newbery and Caldecott winners are selected by two committees of the Association for Library Service to Children, a division of the American Library Association (ALA).

The John Newbery Medal, the oldest award for children's books, was established in 1922. The ALA annually awards the Newbery Medal, named for eighteenth-century British bookseller John Newbery, to the author of the most distinguished contribution to American literature for children. This award is the most prestigious in children's literature. Books may also receive recognition as Newbery Honor books. These books are runners-up to the medal-winning book.

The Randolph J. Caldecott Medal is named in honor of a great English illustrator of the nineteenth century, Randolph Caldecott. The Caldecott Medal was established in 1938. The ALA annually awards the Caldecott Medal to the artist of the most distinguished American picture book for children. Books may also receive recognition as Caldecott Honor Books. These books are runners-up to the medal-winning book.

Educators must recognize that Newbery and Caldecott award-winning books are an essential part of every classroom. These books are appropriate for all grade levels, cover many subjects, contain character principles, and stimulate and motivate children. Although the Newbery and Caldecott seals do not automatically make a book perfect for the classroom, educators can be assured that most of these books have both high-quality text and exquisite illustrations. There are several other awards for a variety of children's literature, too. When educators, parents, and caregivers have to choose literature for their classroom or at home, they must look to the list of winners as a guide.

Educators must therefore acquaint children with some of the medal-winning books and their authors and illustrators. Many schools have competitions for children to read the most award-winning books in a month. See appendix G for a list of the Newbery Medal books and appendix H for a list of the Caldecott Medal books.

The Children's Book Committee, founded almost one hundred years ago, also compiles one of the most comprehensive annotated book lists for children. This list can help educators, parents, caregivers, and librarians choose books that children will find captivating and transforming. It reviews more than six thousand titles each year for accuracy and literary quality and considers their emotional impact on children. The committee chooses the best six hundred books, both fiction and nonfiction, which it lists with annotations, according to age and category.

Educators must also familiarize children with some of these books, and share the list with parents and caregivers. These books can be accessed online at Bankstreet—Best Books of the Year (http://www.bnkst.edu/cbc/best-books2011). Also available online and in most local libraries is *The Best Children's Books of the Year 2009: Hundredth Anniversary Edition*, which features the best children's book from 1900 to 2000 and beyond.

PICTURE BOOKS

Picture books—a format for a book and not a genre—are the principal format through which early learners experience literature. Picture books are illustrated books in which the pictures are essential for early learners to completely understand and enjoy the story. Picture books are also frequently visualized as books in which the text is written at a level that early learners understand but cannot yet read.

Picture books are varied in form and format. They consist of books in text and verse, fiction and nonfiction, big books and little books, board books, concept books (teaching an alphabet or counting), pattern books, and wordless books. They are also cloth books, pop-up books, and books with moving parts. Basically, picture books are used for all ages, though picture books are most suitable for pre-readers ages birth to five years old.

Picture books tell stories through pictures, either alone or combined with text. The content of the book is either fully explained or illustrated with pictures. In a picture book story, the illustrations are as significant as the words, and the two work together to tell the story. With repeated exposure to books, early learners become aware that with the pictures, there are sentences in books. Early learners gain a great deal of knowledge from pictures; consequently, it is important that educators, parents, and caregivers use picture books to teach early learners to read images.

Picture books are also fun for nonreading early learners. Children often tell a story in a picture book based on the illustrations, pretending to read the book. As a result, educators, parents, and caregivers must read picture books aloud to early learners. Visually attractive illustrations in picture books excite and surprise early learners and fill them with a host of ideas, words, and questions. Again, colorful and intriguing illustrations attract the attention of early learners and get them excited about stories, pictures, and ultimately reading. Most importantly, illustrations are key ways early learners convey and develop meaning and recall new vocabulary, because early learners look for hints and details in the illustrations as they are reading for help with the vocabulary.

When reading picture books to early learners, educators, parents, and caregivers must emphasize elements of both the text and pictures. They must also discuss the story's content, introduce the author or authors and illustrator, display the cover of the book, and analyze the story. These details lure early learners into stories by capturing and maintaining their interest and enjoyment. In addition, such details allow them to make connections between their life understandings and the contents of the books. Early learners must be challenged to pay attention to a detail within the book—for example, what can be inferred about the character during the story. Hold the book so that children notice the pictures; if not, read each page and then show the related picture. Pause at predetermined points and pose questions about the story.

Picture books are excellent tools that support emerging reading skills. There is a direct link between the pictures and the text. The text enhances the meanings of the pictures. Pictures without the text can still tell the story; however, words add details. They help children develop concepts about books and print, phonological awareness, vocabulary learning, reading fluency, and reading comprehension. Paving the way for higher reading, picture books are a link to chapter books, which are introduced to early learners in later grades. Textbox 4.1 shows a few award-winning picture books for children.

TEXTBOX 4.1 AWARD-WINNING PICTURE BOOKS

➤ *Owl Moon*, written by Jane Yolen and illustrated by John Schoenher (Caldecott Medal Book)
➤ *The Snowy Day*, written and illustrated by Ezra Jack Keats (Caldecott Medal Book)
➤ *The Little House*, written by Virginia Lee Burton (Caldecott Medal Book)

EASY READER BOOKS

Easy reader books are also sometimes called beginning reader books or early reader books. These books are aimed at early learners beginning to read and are appropriate for children ages five through seven years old. Easy reader books help early learners make the transition from having picture books read to them, to reading chapter books on their own. Easy reader books vary in length but often contain 1,000 to 2,500 words.

Easy reader books can have an adult appearance and use controlled rhythmic patterns and picture clues as a means of presenting high-frequency words for mastery. The focus of easy reader books is to expose children to the one hundred most frequently used words. They generally contain an introductory page filled with words early learners will see in the book. Educators, parents, and, caregivers need to be aware of these words so that they can emphasize them as the child reads the books.

Because of the targeted age of easy reader books, they are grammatically simple, the sentences are short, and the language is familiar to early learners. Nonetheless, a number of easy readers contain some difficult words to challenge early learners. This challenge gives children the opportunity to practice using context clues and other reading skills to determine the meanings of the words.

Easy reader books are great for building basic vocabularies. They provide context for new words to encourage children as they learn to read.

There are many easy reader series and multiple reading levels. Educators must educate parents and caregivers how to distinguish appropriate books based on their children's reading level and personal interests. Textbox 4.2 shows a few good easy reader books for children.

TEXTBOX 4.2 EASY READER BOOKS

➢ *Arthur's Family Vacation: An Arthur Adventure*, written by Marc Brown
➢ *The Berenstain Bears Down on the Farm*, written and illustrated by Jan and Stan Berenstain
➢ *PJ Funnybunny Camps Out*, written by Marilyn Sadler and illustrated by Roger Bollen

---

CHAPTER BOOKS

Chapter books create more challenges for early learners than picture books and easy reader books. These books continue to stimulate children to get involved in reading. As early learners progress from shared and guided reading to independent reading, they need books that support their efforts. Chapter books are written for children who are moving toward reading independently. These books are divided into chapters, and they typically have less picture support than picture books, more demanding language, more complex characters, multiple plot strands, and are greater in length.

The starting point for chapter books usually reflects an early learner's maturity and language proficiency. Short chapter books are appropriate for children ages seven to nine years old, and longer chapter books are appropriate for children ages nine to eleven years old. Chapter books tend to appeal to readers of all ages, because they often feature age-appropriate central characters. Early learners at this stage need to learn story language and language structure, so these elements must be included in introductory chapter books; such books must have an expected sense of story, along with situations to which the reader relates.

To be ready for chapter books, children should be able to do the following:

- Listen for more than thirty minutes of reading aloud from picture books
- Enjoy the text as much as the pictures
- Relate to the characters and follow more complex picture books
- Ask for favorite books to be read repeatedly
- Demonstrate an increased understanding of written language and ask questions.

To select beginning chapter books, consider the number of chapters in the book and the number of pages in each chapter. Chapters need to be divided to support the story structure. To strengthen the correct use of chapter books at home, educators need to share the following approaches with parents and caregivers:

- After reading the title or the first page of the book, ask children what questions they have.
- Preselect a short passage to read to children as a motivator to learn more.
- Share a story about the author.
- Have children keep journals in which they answer specific questions or express their overall feelings about the book while reading.
- Ask children to visualize characters and settings.
- Allow children to discuss reactions to the book.
- Occasionally ask questions to boost children's interest and comprehension.
- Have children take turns reading sections.
- After they read the book, encourage children to share their impressions, feelings, and views about the book.
- Make the book available for children who wish to read it independently.

Textbox 4.3 shows a few good chapter books for children.

TEXTBOX 4.3 CHAPTER BOOKS

➢ *Curious George*, written and illustrated by Margret and H. A. Rey
➢ *Nate the Great*, written by Marjorie Sharmat and illustrated by Marc Simont
➢ *Henry and Mudge*, written by Cynthia Rylant and illustrated by Sucie Stevenson

---

NONFICTION BOOKS

Despite the *non* in the term *nonfiction*, what nonfiction does is more important than what it does not do. What does it do? Nonfiction documents and celebrates the real world, which means everything about the real world that is actual, observable, recordable, demonstrable, and "experienceable," according to Alan Tressell-Cullen (1999).

Nonfiction books are sometimes referred to as informational books. These books give facts on a variety of subjects and are designed to help early learners learn more about the real world. They are written by experts in their fields or by writers who study a subject and compile the facts on a particular subject. Nonfiction books inform and entertain early learners by presentation, illustration, and research. Moreover, nonfiction books build background knowledge, increase vocabulary, and enrich the use of text for early learners.

Nonfiction appeals to readers of both genders and all ages. Many reading specialists and librarians believe that there is not enough nonfiction for early learners. Studies reveal that many children who are not interested in fiction might become motivated readers if introduced to appropriate nonfiction. Another research study found that when more nonfiction text is included in first-grade classrooms, it fosters in children better attitudes toward reading.

Educators must share the following approaches with parents and caregivers for the use of nonfiction books with early learners:

- Spend sufficient time and inform early learners about how nonfiction books are organized. In particular, early learners must be taught to identify the table of contents, index, headings, sidebars, and glossary.
- When reading nonfiction books with children, parents and caregivers need to browse through the pages and notice what grabs their children's attention. In addition, the adults need to ask the children what they notice in the illustrations, what they know about the topic, and what further information they need to learn.
- Ask children questions so that children draw inferences, apply background knowledge, or ponder issues. It is more beneficial to question children at the end of a paragraph or chapter. Questions draw children into discussions.
- Combine reading with hands-on experiences, such as a hands-on craft project or dramatic play props. These activities promote a richer discussion of the text and build knowledge and motivation.
- Make reading-writing connections. These connections are great tools in working with nonfiction texts and early learners. By writing about individual texts, early learners think more about the features of the text and the reading process. Early readers could express their thinking through drawing pictures.

The language in some nonfiction books may contain unfamiliar sentence structures for early learners. Children practice their reading skills to decode the meanings of these sentences. Nonetheless, nonfiction books create a balance between the need for information and the art of storytelling, so early learners need time and familiarity to gain greater understanding of nonfiction books.

Educators, parents, and caregivers must base the evaluation of a nonfiction book on the accuracy of the information as well as the presentation of the information. The material must be organized in a logical manner, and the author must present the material appropriately. Also, influential adults need to take time and learn about nonfiction literature and how to help early learners reach their full reading achievement.

Nonfiction literature stimulates children's awareness by allowing them to learn important reading vocabulary and interesting information, which inspires children to recognize that reading is a valuable skill. Nonfiction literature is known to place demands on early learners who are learning to read; nevertheless, nonfiction literature furnishes early learners with the skills and eagerness to become independent readers. Textbox 4.4 shows a few good nonfiction books for children.

TEXTBOX 4.4 NONFICTION BOOKS

➢ *First the Egg*, written by Laura Vaccaro Seeger (Caldecott Honor Book)
➢ *Remember: The Journey to School Integration*, written by Toni Morrison
➢ *Balloons Over Broadway: The True Story of the Puppeteer of Macy's Parade*, written and illustrated by Melissa Sweet (Caldecott Honor Book)

FICTION

Fiction is the most popular type of children's literature. These books are imaginary and are used for pleasure reading. Safer than nonfiction books, fiction allows readers to remain distant and disconnected from unsettling material. Because fiction books are imaginary, discussing make-believe characters, settings, and circumstances can be emotionally easier. Typically, influential people choose fiction books for the first ones to read aloud to early learners, because of their appealing qualities. One kind of fiction is realistic fiction, in which the plots, characters, and settings are found in real life. They describe stories that could occur. Divided into three kinds of fiction, contemporary, historical, and science fiction, contemporary fiction focuses on current affairs or the recent past. Historical fiction takes place in a time remote enough to be considered history. Science fiction, another type of fiction, usually takes place in the future.

Contemporary fiction is the most popular of all genres of children's literature. Describing stories established in modern times that do not bring in any features of make-believe, they examine a problem that could occur in anybody's life. They concern family situations, peer relationships, growth and maturity, and acceptance of cultural differences. In spite of dealing with everyday problems, realistic fiction does not have to be serious or controversial. Contemporary fiction usually focuses on making the literature as realistic as possible.

Historical fiction takes place in a time and place in the past. It portrays events that actually occurred or possibly could have occurred. Likewise, the plot and characters are created by the writer in a historical setting with interesting stories. Early learners learn about the world in the past. It allows early learners the opportunities to live vicariously in times and places they cannot experience any other way. Some historical fiction stories provide lived-in experiences. These experiences encourage early learners to care for and appreciate others who are different from them. Ranging from stories established in prehistoric times to stories that reflect the issues and events of the current century, historical fiction covers a wide range of topics.

Science fiction is a type of modern fantasy (discussed in traditional literature). Operating outside the normal limits of the real world, these books are usually set in the future. Stories in science fiction combine fact and fiction with innovative technology. The magic of science fiction is the exploration of scientific fact. It often poses ethical questions about current scientific trends and predictions. Children focus on the adventure of exploring the unknown and the wonder of discovering new worlds and peoples. Science fiction speculates on a world that might one day become possible. Relevant in today's rapidly changing world, science fiction makes science palatable to early learners and can pique their interests in the subject.

Fiction books captivate early learners and expand their imaginations. The story mode brings characters to life. It allows children to envision other settings and times. Further, fiction books absorb children in the lives of others and touch familiar subjects shared by everyone. Early learners experience their world and find meaning in their lives through the stories in their everyday connections with the world and in those captured in the literature.

The following are recommendations for educators, parents, and caregivers:

- Always begin with enjoyable books. To enhance the reading experience, pre-read the book before sharing it with children.
- Provide background information on the topic before reading the book to children. This information lets children build their knowledge framework and gather information from previous understanding. It also stimulates discussion about the topic.
- Draw attention to the author, illustrator, and publisher of the book and comment on the correctness of the information.
- Do not read all fiction books to children from cover to cover. Read only one chapter, a small section, or several passages from the book, and then encourage children to read the remainder. Textbox 4.5 shows a few good contemporary, historical, and science fiction books for children.

TEXTBOX 4.5 CONTEMPORARY, HISTORICAL, AND SCIENCE FICTION BOOKS

Contemporary Fiction

➤ *The Red Book,* written by Barbara Lehman (Caldecott Honor Book)
➤ *What Do You Do with a Tail Like This?,* written by Steve Jenkins and Robin Page (Caldecott Honor Book)
➤ *Nancy Drew Starter Set,* written by Carolyn Keene

Historical Fiction

➤ *Crispin: The Cross of Lead,* written by Avi (Newbery Medal Book)
➤ *Hot Air: The (Mostly) True Story of the First Hot Air Balloon Ride,* written and illustrated by Marjorie Priceman (Caldecott Honor Book)
➤ *Adam of the Road,* written by Elizabeth Janet Gray and illustrated by Robert Lawson (Newbery Medal Book)

Science Fiction

➤ *Seven Blind Mice,* written by Ed Young (Caldecott Honor Book)
➤ *So You Want to Be President,* written by Judith St. George and illustrated by David Small (Caldecott Medal Book)
➤ *Flotsam,* written by David Wiesner

TRADITIONAL LITERATURE

Traditional literature is a type of children's literature in which the stories are passed down from one generation to another, sometimes by word of mouth. These stories do not generally have a known originating author and often begin with "Once upon a time . . . ." Traditional literature originates in oral form, but many stories are written down. These stories consist primarily of poems, short stories, and songs that fall into several overlapping categories.

Traditional literature shares these features:

• No identified authors
• Brief stories with simple and direct plots
• Focused and fast-paced action, which adds interest
• Unimportant setting
• Limited themes, such as good versus evil and right versus wrong
• Happy endings
• Magic accepted as normal

There are many forms of traditional literature, as the following list shows:

- Myths are stories that explain something about the world and in-volve gods or other supernatural beings. These stories include hu-man relationships with gods, gods' relationships with each other, and human struggle with good and evil. These stories can contain action, suspense, and conflict, and are religious in their origin.
- Legends are similar to myths and are deeply rooted in the histories of particular places or cultures. The stories are based on history, but exaggerate the life of a real person. The facts and adventures of the person are embellished. Because legends are stories and are passed down through generations, the actual truth is questionable.
- Epics are long narratives in verse that tell about the adventure of a hero or some historical events. An epic can be a subcategory of a myth. For example, an epic has a hero who symbolizes all ideal characteristics of that particular time, such as Robin Hood, who represented justice and freedom of a society. The knowledge of epics allows early learners to understand other cultures.
- Tall tales are stories characterized by exaggerated details, and the main character is larger than life and has an explicit job. There is a conflict in the story, and it is resolved in a humorous manner. Over-stated details define the characters, settings, and events.
- Fables are short stories that teach a moral lesson, and they usually have animals that act like humans. The themes and characters appeal to early learners, and the stories are often humorous and entertaining for children.
- Ballads are folk rhymes told in song form, but they are poems with a strong narrative structure. Typical topics are a sad death, a tragic romance, or a stirring and dramatic adventure of a hero. A tradi-tional ballad has a regular rhythm and includes plenty of repetition. Some lines are repeated word for word or in a lightly changed form, similar to a refrain of a song.
- Nursery rhymes are a form of short ballad. People commonly tell nursery rhymes to children. The rhymes tend to be humorous in content, and they teach a lesson.
- Folktales are written or oral and have been passed down over the years by word of mouth. They are culturally influenced and are often based on human behaviors. The majority of traditional lit-erature consists of folktales that convey the legends, customs, su-perstitions, and beliefs of people in past times. Folktales provide children with an opportunity to discover the universal qualities of humankind. A popular type of folktale is the fairy tale, which usu-ally concerns magic, enchanted creatures, a sense of good eventu-

ally overcoming evil, and characters such as witches, sorcerers, and talking animals.

- Fairy tales usually originate in written form. Fairy tales include a magical element and show rich and poor, good and evil, reward and punishment. They involve enchanted places where all things are possible and end happily. The magical element can include fantastic creatures such as trolls, unicorns, ogres, or animals personified. In fairy tales, things often happen to royalty as an outcome of a spell or curse. Fairy tales have been collected by known authors, such as Charles Perrault, and also authors such as the Grimm brothers, who wrote the tales as a way to document and entertain their lives.
- Religious stories have features of traditional literature, although most people do not classify religious stories with traditional literature. Some people believe that classifying them together implies that religious stories are fictionalized, like myths, and that they denounce religion. Religious tales have features of traditional literature, however. Tunnell and Jacobs (2000) stated that religious tales involved a "human's quest to discover and share with one another the truth concerning the spiritual aspects of existence" (p. 72), which were first told through oral storytelling.
- Modern fantasy is rooted in traditional literature, and it has an identifiable author. In modern fantasy, the events, settings, or the characters are outside the realm of possibility. The stories of modern fantasy are imaginative, and there are contemporary fairy tales and stories of magic, talking toys, talking animals, and other wonders or magical powers. Fantasy stories often involve journeys and quests with an end goal or location. The stories of modern fantasy help early learners develop their imagination. They stretch the early learners' imagination and present the world in a different perspective. The author of these books must provide strong characters and explain the fantastical world in great detail in order for children to suspend disbelief and believe in the magic.

Educators, parents, and caregivers must be mindful when selecting traditional literature for early learners to read. Research indicates that for traditional literature to be enjoyable to early learners, it must

- be appropriate for the age, interests, and prior knowledge of the child;
- fit the attention span of the child;
- include an appropriate amount of text in the story;
- contain features of traditional literature, such as a satisfying ending;
- ensure that the writing stays true to the oral storytelling style;
- inspire children's creativity through artistic expression, such as drama, arts, and crafts;

- help the child understand the world and its cultural traditions;
- show connections between similar stories around the world, such as the story of Cinderella, which is found in many cultures;
- teach children to appreciate culture and art from other countries;
- portray cultures accurately; and
- acknowledge the goodness, compassion, bravery, and human struggles of people from other countries.

Traditional literature provides a link between the past and the future. Furthermore, it is an ideal type of literature for teaching early learners about other eras, cultures, and traditions. Equally important is that traditional literature captivates early learners and inspires them to read. Textboxes 4.6, 4.7, and 4.8 show a few good traditional literature books for children.

TEXTBOX 4.6 TRADITIONAL LITERATURE BOOKS

Myths

➤ *Golem*, written and illustrated by David Wisniewski (Caldecott Medal Book)
➤ *The Ugly Duckling*, written by Christian Andersen and illustrated by Jerry Pinkney (Caldecott Honor Book)
➤ *One Fine Day*, written and illustrated by Noni Hogrogian

Legends

➤ *The Tooth Fairy Legend*, written by John Arthur Long and Chet Meyer and illustrated by Chet Meyer
➤ *Legend of Freedom*, written by Lind Jacobs Altman
➤ *Scooby Doo and the Legend of the Vampire*, written by Jessie Leon McCann and illustrated by Duendes Del Sur

Epics

➤ *Saint George and the Dragon*, written by Margaret Hodges and illustrated by Trina Schart Hyman (Caldecott Medal Book)
➤ *The Story of Robin Hood*, retold by Robert Leeson and illustrated by Barbara Lofthouse
➤ *The Adventures of Marco Polo*, written and illustrated by Dieter Wiesmuller

Tall Tales

➤ *John Henry*, written by Julius Lester and illustrated by Jerry Pinkney (Caldecott Honor Book)
➤ *Swamp Angel*, written by Anne Issacs and illustrated by Paul O. Zelinsky (Caldecott Honor Book)
➤ *Holes*, written by Louis Sachar (Newbery Medal Book)

TEXTBOX 4.7 TRADITIONAL LITERATURE BOOKS

Ballads

➢ *Casey at Bat: A Ballad of the Republic Sung in the Year 1888*, written by Ernest L. Thayer and illustrated by Christopher Bing (Caldecott Honor Book)
➢ *Ballad of the Pirate Queens*, written by Jane Yolen and illustrated by David Shannon
➢ *The Ballads of Lucy Whipple*, written by Karen Cushman

Fables

➢ *Fables*, written by Arnold Lobel (Caldecott Medal Book)
➢ *Frog and Toad Are Friends*, written by Arnold Lobel (Caldecott Honor Book)
➢ *Whittington*, written by Alan Armstrong and illustrated by S. D. Schindler (Newbery Medal Book)

Nursery Rhymes

➢ *White Snow, Bright Snow*, written by Alvin Tresselt and illustrated by Roger Duvoisin (Caldecott Medal Book)
➢ *The Rooster Crows: A Book of American Rhymes and Jingles*, written by Maud Fuller Petersham and Miska Petersham (Caldecott Medal Book)
➢ *Mother Goose and Nursery Rhymes*, illustrated by Philip Reed (Caldecott Honor Book)

Folktales

➢ *Strega Nona: An Old Tale Retold*, written and illustrated by Tomie de Paola (Caldecott Honor Book)
➢ *Three Billy-Goats Gruff (Easy-To-Read Folktale)*, written and illustrated by Ellen Appleby

---

BIOGRAPHY

In children's literature, biography often bridges the gap between historical fiction and informational books. Biographical books introduce early learners to the concept of nonfiction. A biography is the true story of a real person's life from the past or present, written by another person. Biographies for early learners are based on the life, or portion of the life, of a real person. Included in biography is autobiography, which is the story of a real person's life written by that same person. Biography and autobiography are sometimes an overlooked genre for children, yet they are a favorite type of literature for many lifetime readers.

TEXTBOX 4.8 TRADITIONAL LITERATURE BOOKS

Folktales

➤ *How Tiger Got His Stripes: A Folktale from Vietman (Story Cove: A World of Stories)*, written by Rob Cleveland and illustrated by Baird Hoffmire

Fairy Tales

➤ *Rumpelstiltskin*, retold and illustrated by Paul O. Zelinsky (Caldecott Honor Book)
➤ *Cinderella*, text translated from Charles Perrault by Marcia Brown and illustrated by Marcia Brown (Caldecott Medal Book)
➤ *The Three Pigs*, written by David Wiesner (Caldecott Medal Book)

Religious Stories

➤ *Noah's Ark*, written by Peter Spier (Caldecott Medal Book)
➤ *Prayer for a Child*, written by Rachel Field and illustrated by Elizabeth Orton Jones (Caldecott Medal Book)
➤ *Animals of the Bible*, written by and illustrated by Dorothy P. Lathrop (Caldecott Medal Book)

Modern Fantasy

➤ *Monster Mama*, written by Liz Rosenberg and illustrated by Stephen Gammell
➤ *Matilda*, written by Roald Dahl and illustrated by Quentin Blake
➤ *Harry Potter: A Pop-up Book: Based on the Film Phenomenon*, written by Lucy Kee, created by Bruce Foster, and illustrated by Andrew Williamson. The text of the book includes a number of behind-the-scenes facts regarding the films from various individuals involved in their creation, including the producers, actors, and J. K. Rowling.

The stories in biographies sometimes read like fiction, but like nonfiction, they center on documented facts and proceedings. Over the years, children's biographies have revealed a wide range of factual orientation, from strict truthfulness to generous fictionalization. The fictionalization of these books occurred because many experts thought that early learners would not read a biography unless it read like a good story. This theory resulted in stories that may be fascinating but inaccurate.

Today biographies are authentic, yet the stories present the subject's life in ways that excite and engage early learners. An authentic biography is a well-documented, carefully researched story of a person's life. In contrast, fictionalized biography documents facts, but the writer dramatizes certain events and personalizes the subjects. Even so, any conceived dialogue or background fact must be credible and true to the times.

Biographical books may pertain to scientists and inventors, political leaders, explorers and frontiersmen, humanitarians, performers (in music, art, and literature), sports personalities, individuals who overcame great odds, villains, and ordinary individuals. Through children's literature, early learners are also exposed to the biographies and contributions of important individuals within the context of important holidays—for example, Martin Luther King Jr.'s birthday. Often the person's life is notable for the person's accomplishments or a significant triumph. The lives documented in biographies let early learners realize how the process of growing up shapes the opportunities, choices, and trials people encounter in their lives.

Children enjoy reading stories about other people. Biographies provide children with a glimpse of the kinds of lives they might choose to live. Biographical books help early learners answer questions that are important to them. These books also raise questions about how children's lives might unfold.

When educators introduce biographical literature, they must educate children on how to get the most out of their reading. The following are a few guidelines educators must share with parents and caregivers to increase their awareness of biographies for early learners:

- They must be informed that the biography opens children's eyes and hearts to people who have made a difference in the world.
- They must be educated on the differences among biographical titles in the same series of books. It must be stressed that individual titles need to be reviewed, not the entire series.
- They must be told to select books with illustrations, because illustrations arouse early learners' interest. A book with only pure content and facts is unlikely to seize an early learner's interest.
- They must be encouraged to come into their child's classroom to help their child during the gathering of information for a biography project. This participation increases a child's interest in the biography project.

Put simply, biographical literature offers early learners a more intimate and memorable quality of knowing. Equally important is that biographies increase an early learner's thirst for knowledge and promote reading achievement. Textbox 4.9 shows a few good biography books for children.

POETRY

Poetry is verse written to capture a feeling, event, or thought. It frequently uses rhyme and rhythm to help deliver its meaning, or it may

---

TEXTBOX 4.9 BIOGRAPHY BOOKS

➤ *Dr. Seuss (First Biographies)*, written by Cheryl Carlson
➤ *Helen Keller (Scholastic Biography)*, written by Margaret Davidson and
  illustrated by Wendy Watson
➤ *Rosa*, written by Nikki Giovanni and illustrated by Bryan Collier (Caldecott
  Honor Book)

---

be presented in free verse. It fulfills an early learner's natural response to rhythm. For example, early learners will sing their vocabulary words and respond to rhyme in poems. Rhyme creates melodic characteristics of a poem, and early learners naturally delight in the sound, rhythm, and language of poetry. Poetry brings early learners pleasure, allows them to notice their world, and develops their awareness.

Poetry includes nursery rhymes, ballads, epics, songs, poems, and lyrics (poetry that sings its way into the minds and memories of its listeners). Because poetry is written at varying reading levels, it can be matched with early learners' interest and abilities. All children must be exposed to poetry in their lives. The rich descriptive language of poetry is pleasing to the ear. Poetry is therefore appropriate for read-aloud books for early learners.

Poetry can introduce factual information to children in a lyrical manner or tell a story using narrative rhyme. By using poetry effectively, educators alter the mood inside a classroom. Poetry can also be used to begin and end lessons and activities. Likewise, poetry may be read at school assemblies or during interactive hours with parents or caregivers. Dramatic poetry readings are often conducted in public places such as bookstores or libraries. These readings, in some cases, are enhanced with props, costumes, sound effects, or background music.

Early learners must be encouraged to perform solo poetry readings. For instance, some early learners like to perform individually in front of parents, caregivers, or peers. Early learners who like to memorize poems must be encouraged to do so, provided they do it willingly and are able to select the poem.

Controversy exists among experts regarding memorizing poems. Some say the burden to recall the words in front of an audience can be harmful to early learners' enjoyment of poetry, because of their anxiety not to forget the words. On the other hand, Michael Knox Beran (2004) notes in the article "In Defense of Memorization" that learning poetry by memory empowers children.

To foster collaboration, educators must instruct parents and caregivers to engage early learners with poetry in the following six ways:

TEXTBOX 4.10 POETRY BOOKS

➤ *I Am Phoenix: Poems for Two Voices*, written by Paul Fleischman and illustrated by Ken Nutt (Newbery Medal Book)
➤ *Song of the Water Boatman and Other Pond Poems*, written by Joyce Sidman and illustrated by Beckie Prange (Caldecott Honor Book)
➤ *Sing a Song of Popcorn: Every Child's Book of Poems*, selected by Beatrice Schenk de Regniers and Eva Moore, illustrated by Caldecott winners

---

1. Have a wide selection of poems to share with early learners.
2. Work with early learners to discover and enjoy poetry together.
3. Emphasize to early learners that poetry is a regular part of schoolwork.
4. Relate poetry to early learners' experiences or classroom activities.
5. Ask early learners questions that contribute to the meaning and enjoyment of a poem.
6. Encourage early learners to memorize poems that they themselves select.

Educators must expose early learners to many forms of poetry. Exposure develops children's understanding and appreciation of the literature. Consequently, early and fun-filled exposure to poetry contributes to an early learner's lifelong love of poetry and reading. Textbox 4.10 shows a few good poetry books for children.

POINTS TO REMEMBER

Children's literature provides early learners with an opportunity to become readers. It is used to do the following:

- Develop or enhance reading skills
- Build knowledge by introducing themes, topics, and messages
- Teach children about their world
- Open children's minds to adventures
- Spark children's imagination
- Keep their interest
- Educate early learners to understand and appreciate their own culture and the culture of others
- Make children want to read

The more early learners read stories, the more they interpret books based on their own background knowledge and share their own ideas and views with others. Children's literature allows early learners to become imaginative, have a wide outlook, and develop positive attitudes toward reading. Children are naturally drawn to stories, and children's literature provides a motivating, meaningful perspective for early learners. Furthermore, children's literature introduces early learners to patterns of language, extends their vocabulary, and improves their comprehension. Ample literature allows children to improve their reading achievement and develop better attitudes toward reading.

When educators, parents, and caregivers read and discuss children's literature with early learners, together they must question the way the world is represented in literature. Over the years, educators have written articles for scholarly journals about their successes with using children's literature in reading programs. These reports confirm that literature promotes success in learning to read. Children's literature also helps early learners discover the pleasure of reading and develop a love for reading.

Children's literature entertains, stretches imaginations, elicits a wealth of emotions, and develops compassion. It generates questions and new knowledge and provides encounters with differing beliefs and values. Educators, parents, and caregivers must help early learners seek out and enjoy experiences with books, become familiar with the language of literature and the patterns of stories, and understand and follow the sequence of stories read to them.

One must always respect each child's selection of books for independent reading. Self-selection is the key to instilling a love of literature and reading. A wide variety of literature provides opportunities for increasing vocabulary and reading comprehension. A variety of captivating choices increases early learners' reading motivation. It is also critical for reluctant or struggling readers to have access to literature that stimulates them. Research indicates that children want to read more often when they are able to choose what they will read and have the opportunity to interact with others to discuss what they have read.

Educators, parents, and caregivers must provide early learners with a superb, rich literature program in their early years for them to be ready to read and to experience the joy and love of reading. Learning to read provides children a valuable tool for acquiring information. Likewise, it allows children to find meaning in the books they read and equips them with an essential set of skills for developing a rich, imaginative, and ever-expanding life. Certainly it is no longer a question of whether early learners read; it is now only a question of what they are going to read.

5

Encouraging Children to Love What They Read

Teaching children to read continues to be a highly investigated area of education, and it is consistently a focus of our nation's initiatives. The NCLB Act requires schools to take steps to make certain that all children are reading at grade level by the end of the third grade. As a result, schools across our nation continually search for ways to achieve this standard.

Substantial research exists for implementing effective interventions in the elementary grades for children with reading difficulties. These interventions sometimes include Reading Recovery (RR), Response to Intervention (RTI or RtI) models, and the Success for All (SFA) programs to be discussed later in this chapter. For the majority of children, these interventions result in significantly improved reading performance over time. They are also the most effective course of action for the prevention of reading failures. Without systematic, focused, and intensive interventions, the majority of struggling readers will not read at grade level. For that reason, well-designed, evidence-based early identification, prevention, and intervention programs are needed in schools.

With prevention and early intervention, experts have found that reading failure in the early years is reduced to fewer than one in ten children. That is, more than nine out of ten children are able to become average, or even above-average, readers. In fact, if educators adopt intervention techniques in the classroom, first graders, who have the greatest reading challenges of all, are able to reach grade-level reading by the end of second grade with intensive, targeted intervention. This pattern also holds true for children whose parents have reading disabilities—although this contingency of children often has a higher rate of reading disabilities, they, too, can achieve grade-level reading comprehension when prevention and intervention methods are instituted in the classroom.

Strategies to prevent academic failure involve creating a school culture dedicated to academic success for all children. Schools can accomplish this goal by providing interventions designed to prevent early failure, to nurture educator and learner relationships, to ensure a relevant and engaging curriculum and good instruction, to allow extra time and extra help for struggling readers, and to seek firm parental involvement.

To demonstrate how educators can best apply intervention techniques in their elementary classrooms, this chapter explains professional development and Literacy First, a type of professional development for educators. It will also delve into the roles of reading specialists, finding children's motivation to read, instituting early intervention programs, adding supplemental comprehensive intervention reading programs, and action steps for educators to take.

PROFESSIONAL DEVELOPMENT
AND LITERACY FIRST FOR EDUCATORS

Professional development generally refers to ongoing learning opportunities available to educators and other education personnel through their schools and districts. Well-trained educators and reading instructions that are based on research deliver the best teaching strategies and programs to all children, particularly in the development of early learners' reading skills.

National reports and government mandates have raised expectations for the formal education and training of early childhood educators. The U.S. Department of Education indicates that it is essential for educators of kindergarten through third-grade children to have additional training, preparation, and use of reading diagnostics. Several states have established pre-kindergarten through third-grade certification programs and launched incentives to encourage educators to elevate and magnify their knowledge and skills. Nevertheless, an educator's education is viewed as an ongoing process, along with continued professional development.

The National Reading Panel (NRP) indicates that educators must fully understand the structure of the English language and the similarities and differences between written and spoken language in order to successfully teach reading. Likewise, researchers at the National Institutes of Health found that only a small percentage of educators are skilled enough to teach reading to children who have reading difficulties. The inadequacy in some educators' training makes it vital that time be given to professional development, which allows educators to advance their knowledge of reading instruction. The early grades must be a learning community for both educators and early learners.

To transform early learners into superb readers, professional development must be perceived as one of the primary vehicles for efforts to bring about change. For educators to reach their full potential, it is important that administrators support their efforts. Professional development involves constant collaboration, reflection, and ongoing support among all participants.

Literacy First, a type of professional development for educators, was established in 1998. It provides educators with effective, easily implemented instructional strategies in reading. Literacy First is a research-based, systematic, and comprehensive reading reform process that accelerates reading achievement of all children from pre-kindergarten to twelfth grade. Literacy First does the following:

➢ Strengthens an educator's knowledge of effective skills and processes and instructs educators in how to teach in a systematic, explicit way to develop comprehension.
➢ Increases the instructional leadership skills of the administration to monitor and support all the critical components for growth in reading achievement of all children.

Literacy First has an instructional content and commitment to ongoing professional development. Integrated is a process to improve reading instruction, irrespective of the school's reading programs. Its purpose is to make educators more knowledgeable and skilled in key instructional elements of phonemic awareness, phonics, fluency, vocabulary development, and comprehension skills. Furthermore, educators learn how best to organize flexible reading groups and how to plan activities that promote the development of reading skills, concepts, and strategies. The program also provides assessment tools for assigning children to reading groups and for monitoring children's progress so that educators advance children as their achievement levels change.

Literacy First provides a comprehensive three-year plan to accelerate reading achievement. It includes the following:

• A concise structured daily plan for children to receive two hours of systematic and explicit reading instruction, plus up to twenty minutes of monitored independent reading practice
• Analysis of a school's current reading program and culture

- Incorporation of the school current curriculum into the literacy plan
- Creation of a three-year strategic plan unique to the individual school
- Training of administrators and educators
- Ongoing on-site professional development, coaching, and consultation for educators and administrators to actualize the reform plan

During the first year, Literacy First provides educators of kindergartners, first graders, and second graders with five days of professional development. In addition, a program representative spends five days at the school coaching and consulting with educators. In the second year, the training continues with three more days of professional development for educators of kindergarten through second grade, and it begins with five days of professional development for third-, fourth-, and fifth-grade educators. During the third and final year, educators from third to fifth grade get three more days of professional development and six more days of coaching and consulting. Additionally, Literacy First includes unlimited coaching and consultation by telephone and e-mail throughout the three-year period.

Administrators must participate in Literacy First for it to be successful. They must accompany their educators to training sessions and attend the leadership institute that Literacy First operates to bring together administrators from several school systems. This system allows administrators to build a network and acquire insights into practices elsewhere. Administrators must also agree to spend an hour a day visiting classrooms. Equally important is that central administrators pledge to devote a minimum of one hour a week in classrooms. Educators and administrators, like children, are also lifelong learners.

Literacy First consultants hold either a master's or doctorate degree and are former or current educators and administrators. Each Literacy First consultant participates in an extensive training process that consists of an initial training and copresenting with an experienced consultant, for which each consultant receives evaluations on every presentation.

Supportive classrooms where children experience success with skilled reading educators are central to helping all children prepare for the literacy demands they will face in society. To advance the reading skills of early learners, very little materializes unless educators, administrators, parents, and caregivers assume the responsibility to make it transpire. Early learners' reading success is not completely realized unless educators and administrators secure the entire essential preparation and make the most of every opportunity to help children learn to read. Literacy First is a great change-implementation process based on a strong site relationship among all participants.

ROLES OF READING SPECIALISTS

All children need excellent reading instruction to learn to read. Educators succeed at teaching children to read when the educators have the knowledge and competence necessary to teach reading effectively. Even so, individuals need specialized knowledge about reading instruction. These individuals provide essential services not only to children, but also to other educators. Children who struggle with reading must obtain additional instruction from professionals specifically prepared to teach them. These professionals are usually reading specialists who serve as advocates for a literacy program.

Reading specialists are professionals with advanced preparation and experience in reading assessment and training. They provide instruction and serve as resources to educators for the literacy performance of all readers, but specifically struggling readers. The majority of reading specialists work in elementary schools, but they also serve an important role in upper-level schools. Reading specialists play an essential role that supports administrators while also being a resource to parents, caregivers, and the community.

Reading specialists lead professional development workshops and suggest ideas, strategies, or materials to educators to improve reading instruction. In addition, reading specialists provide instructional guidance to aides, volunteer tutors, or paraprofessionals who may work in classrooms to assist educators in meeting the needs of children. Having a key role in building effective school-home connections, they work with parents and caregivers and other educators to establish effective educator-parent relationships.

Reading specialists work in various settings, such as public or private facilities, reading-resource centers, clinics, and community tutoring centers. In schools, some reading specialists work primarily in a teaching role with children. Some spend the majority of their time in professional development with other educators, in a more formal leadership role. All reading specialists, however, regardless of their role or the settings in which they work, must work collaboratively with a child's educator to reinforce and support effective classroom instruction. Reading specialists also conduct testing to determine if a child has a reading problem, or if the child possesses the ability but is unmotivated.

The International Reading Association (2010), which provides standards for reading, reveals the following essentials for the reading specialist certification:

- A valid teaching certificate
- Previous teaching experience

- A master's degree with a concentration in reading and writing education
- Program experiences that build knowledge, skills, and dispositions related to working with children, supporting or coaching educators, and leading the school reading program

In addition, there must be the equivalent of twenty-one to twenty-seven graduate semester hours in reading, language arts, and related courses, and the program must include a supervised practicum experience, usually the equivalent of six semester hours. The supervised practicum experience requires working with children who struggle with reading. Also, there must be collaborative and coaching experiences with educators. Again, reading specialists need to have prior classroom experience so that they have a thorough understanding of classroom instruction and a sense of and appreciation for an educator's role. The International Reading Association affirms that every elementary school should have reading specialists.

The National Research Council, in its report "Preventing Reading Difficulties in Young Children," stated that schools without reading specialists need to reexamine their needs. Reading specialists provide leadership and instructional expertise for the prevention and remediation of reading difficulties so that all children can become successful readers. For a more effective reading program, reading specialists must communicate with educators, counselors, parents, caregivers and specialized personnel, such as a special education educator.

Reading specialists provide knowledgeable instruction, assessment, and leadership for a reading program. Moreover, they have a strong influence on the overall reading program in a school and are key factors that improve children's reading achievement. Equally important is for reading specialists to know how to motivate children to become independent learners. The development of children's reading skills affects not only their reading achievement, but also their attitudes and motivation to read.

CHILDREN'S MOTIVATION TO READ

A child's motivation to read can be defined as the cluster of personal goals, values, and beliefs regarding topics, processes, and outcomes of reading that an individual possesses. Because the early years offer the best opportunity for early learners to learn to read, it is vital that children become self-motivated during this period. Educators must share with parents and caregivers that a self-motivated child who encounters difficulty reading frequently succeeds in reading.

Effectiveness in the early grades comes from boosting and fostering motivation, which can strengthen intellectual curiosity and promote more vigorous learning in early learners. Motivation is directly related to a child's success in school. Educators must reward diligence during the early grades as a way to encourage children to strive for their best. Children will eventually discover that success in school requires an increasing amount of persistence. Early learners' experiences in their early years produce significant and often lasting results that have serious, lifelong implications for motivation.

Research indicates that there are ways to increase a child's motivation for reading. For example, offering a variety of materials gives readers a broad choice of genres. Likewise, variety increases motivation, especially when incorporated with technology and visual media. Also, a child's self-selection of text enhances the child's motivation, because it lets him or her make personal connections. Early learners who are more skilled at reading and have a love of reading are more likely to be motivated and successful in their reading achievement; however, an early learner who loses motivation can lose self-confidence and become apprehensive about reading. Therefore, the children's development of self-confidence and realization that they can learn to read motivates them to greater achievement.

Educators also influence the degree to which early learners are motivated. Often educators knowingly and unknowingly send signals to children by facial expressions, body language, and verbal feedback. It is vital to send positive signals to children to nurture their motivation to read. Equally important is parental involvement in increasing the motivation of their children to read. Research continually reveals that the positive influence of parents and caregivers, such as talking with their children about school, checking and helping children with homework, reading aloud, and partaking in activities such as trips to the library, promotes literacy growth and interest.

EARLY INTERVENTION PROGRAMS

The term "early intervention" refers to school intervention programs designed to prevent reading difficulties for many early learners. In the primary grades, children with reading difficulties may need intervention to prevent future reading failure. Early recognition of children who need intervention has become a key factor in the prevention of reading difficulties. Kindergarten is often the first opportunity educators have to provide instruction and assess children's responsiveness. As a result, several early interventions target first graders.

Intervention programs that support the academic achievement of children encourage comprehensive one-on-one strategies, such as tutoring. Researchers confirm that one-on-one tutoring is a very effective strategy for improving reading performance, even in a child's later years. Tutoring provides children with necessary skills for academic success. One-on-one tutoring provides direct, explicit, and systematic instruction responsive to the knowledge and interests of the child experiencing reading difficulties. Tutors can include educators, adult volunteers, peers, homework hotlines, franchised learning centers, clinics, and private agencies.

Some educators, parents, and caregivers do not pursue tutoring, because of time and financial obligations. Nevertheless, schools can provide free tutoring to children through early intervention programs or after-school programs. Some private organizations provide free tutoring to parents and caregivers for their children, based on the guardians' inability to pay for services.

A careful analysis of tutoring programs reveals that regardless of the strategy used, programs that focus on phonics obtain much better results than those that do not. Furthermore, educators must focus on their own teaching skills; and through professional development, they can learn helpful classroom instruction that benefits every child. Research-based instruction and skilled educators are key factors in teaching children to read in the early grades.

The program that a school selects depends on the characteristics of the school's needs. Reading Recovery (RR), Response to Intervention (RtI), and the Success for All (SFA) are programs that help educators identify children in need of intervention and implement evidence-based intervention to promote their reading success. Educators must inform parents and caregivers that they may encounter other tutoring programs, such as Early Steps, Book Buddies, Reading One-to-One, The Howard Street Tutoring Program, The Intergenerational Reading Program, and Help One Student to Succeed (HOSTS). If interested, parents and caregivers must talk to their child's educator and reading specialist for additional details regarding these programs.

Reading Recovery (RR)

Reading Recovery (RR) is a widely used preventive and early intervention program designed for early learners who have failed after a year to respond adequately to formal reading instruction. It has consistently demonstrated success in helping struggling first graders become independent readers. Many schools use RR as a first-grade early intervention for children who are struggling readers. The program was developed in the 1970s by a New Zealand educator, Dr. Marie Clay, from her research in classrooms and clinics, as well as intensive studies from other disciplines. Since 1984, it has been used in most states in the United States. The goal of RR is to significantly decrease the occurrence of reading failure, reduce the number of first-grade children who are struggling to read, and prevent long-term reading difficulties. To identify struggling children, educators rely on assessments from kindergarten educators and children's performance on the Observation Survey of Early Literacy Achievement. This survey has a strong research base, with a battery of six tasks: letter identification, word test, concepts about print, writing vocabulary, hearing and recording sounds in words, and text level reading.

RR supplements regular classroom reading instruction. It involves a series of lessons that have one-to-one instruction by a specially trained educator for thirty to forty minutes a day for twelve to twenty weeks. Over the course of lessons, children read books. These books include two to three familiar ones, a rereading of the previous day's new book, and the introduction and reading of a new story. Educators keep a record of a child's previous book read to analyze his or her independence and reading behavior. Children also compose, write, and read their own messages or stories. Additionally, children read a new text each day.

Within each lesson, RR educators attend to all of the essential components of reading, including phonemic awareness and phonics. Educators give specific and explicit attention to letters, sounds, and words. Educators also help children learn to use connections between letters and sounds, so early learners use their knowledge of how words work to solve problems with difficult words while retaining comprehension.

At the end of the RR, there are two possible outcomes for a child:

1. The series of lessons is discontinued because the child is performing at or near average levels of his or her peers.
2. A recommendation is made to provide the child with additional literacy support based on needs.

RR is a highly effective short-term intervention for struggling first graders. The one-on-one teaching enables the educator to design each lesson to meet the unique needs of each struggling reader without wasting time on what the child has already learned. The intervention is not an alternative to effective classroom teaching, however. Instead, it is complementary and allows children to engage in their classroom program.

Early intervention produces more proficient readers when the RR educator, the classroom educator, parents, and caregivers work collectively. All educators must support each other and collaborate with parents and caregivers so they can continue to support their child's efforts at home. Professional development for those who work with children through RR is an essential part of RR, and it begins with an academic year of graduate-level study and continues in subsequent years.

The What Works Clearinghouse (2007), a government agency that independently evaluates reports on educational programs and interventions, released a report of twenty-four reading intervention programs that had research support. RR was the only one found to have positive effects in all areas reviewed: alphabetics, fluency, comprehension, and general reading achievement. In addition, educators reveal that RR is among the best evidence of the direct link between good design and education excellence.

Response to Intervention (RtI) Models

Response to Intervention (commonly abbreviated RTI or RtI) is a comprehensive early detection and prevention strategy that involves research-based instruction and intervention to provide systematic assistance to children who are have difficulty learning to read. RTI methods combine universal screening and high-quality instruction for all children, with interventions targeted at struggling children.

RTI was originally recognized in the 1970s as a method of identifying children with learning disabilities; however, RTI has become increasingly common, partly because of the 2004 reauthorization of the Individuals with Disabilities Education Act (IDEA). The IDEA encourages states to use RTI to prevent reading difficulties and identify children with learning disabilities. The RTI model provides services and interventions to children at increasing levels of intensity, based on progress monitoring and data analysis.

Parental involvement is crucial to the success of an RTI program. A parent or caregiver helps create an effective RTI program by providing a unique perspective on a child that may not be evident to the educator in the classroom. Consequently, parents and caregivers must be included in the RTI process at the beginning of the program. Parental involvement may include parent-educator conferences or regularly scheduled meetings.

Research indicates that RTI is effective in improving overall reading outcomes and decreasing the number of children with reading difficulties in elementary grades. RTI is a multitiered approach. Several states and school districts have implemented the multitiered intervention systems with more than three tiers. Although RTI models vary, they typically have three tiers. Each tier is defined by specific characteristics.

Tier I: Universal Intervention

1. All children are universally screened.
2. The curriculum is research based.

3. Ongoing assessment and progress monitoring are used to modify curriculum according to children's needs.

Tier I serves as the first intervention provided to all children in the classroom. Children who fail to respond to the core curriculum of Tier I receive additional services under Tier II.

Tier II: Targeted Intervention

1. Children whose performance falls behind peers receive increasingly targeted interventions.
2. Children's progress is closely monitored, and intervention is modified according to children's needs.
3. Parents and caregivers are consulted and informed of their child's response to specific interventions.
4. Educators working in Tier II receive training to deliver a research-based intervention curriculum.

Tier II interventions are provided only to children who demonstrate problems based on screening measures or weak progress from regular classroom instruction. In addition to the general classroom instruction, Tier II children receive supplemental, small-group reading instruction targeted at building foundational reading skills. Children who require a more intensive approach because of unsatisfactory progress in Tier II receive additional intensive or individual interventions.

Tier III: Intensive or Individual Intervention

1. Children are provided with specialized, individual instruction that includes more intensive instruction and smaller group size.
2. Children's progress is monitored daily, and intervention is modified according to children's needs.
3. Specialists provide individual services as needed.
4. Children whose performance does not improve when provided with increasingly intensive instruction are referred to the school's Child Study Team to determine whether they are eligible for special education or related services. Parents and caregivers are consulted during this process.

Tier III interventions are provided to children who do not progress after a reasonable amount of time with the Tier II intervention and require more intensive assistance. Tier III usually entails one-on-one tutoring with a mix of instructional interventions. Ongoing analysis of the child's performance data is critical in Tier III. Systematically collected data are used to identify successes and failures in instruction for individual children. If children continue to have reading difficulties after receiving intensive services, they are evaluated for possible special education services.

Understanding and successfully implementing the RTI process takes time. The initiative requires collaboration among administrators, general educators, special educators, and other educational specialists. The RTI leadership team must also educate and involve parents and caregivers. For example, the RTI leadership team must form parent leadership teams and explain to them the RTI process and terminologies that are sometimes unfamiliar to some parents and caregivers. Nevertheless, it is also the responsibility of a child's educator to educate parents and caregivers and discuss the intervention process with them.

RTI prevents academic failure through early intervention, regular monitoring of children's progress, and increasingly intensive research-based instructional interventions for children who continue to have difficulty. Children who do not respond to effective interventions are likely to have biologically based learning disabilities and to be in need of special education services.

Professional development in RTI must be considered a function of the educational process along with schedules, structures for collaboration, curriculum selection, and instructional leadership. When RTI is implemented with commitment, it creates improved success in academics, more accurate identification of learning disabilities, better attendance rates, higher graduation rates, lower dropout rates, and fewer discipline referrals.

Success for All (SFA)

The Success for All (SFA) program involves a comprehensive reading component designed as a prevention and early intervention for kindergarten through third-grade children. Its underlying premise is that all children can and should be reading at grade level by the end of third grade. The SFA program emphasizes phonemic awareness, vocabulary enrichment, sound blending, and storytelling and retelling techniques. Johns Hopkins University researcher Bob Slavin and his wife, Nancy Madden, both former special education educators, developed the original model of SFA in the 1980s.

SFA calls for a daily ninety-minute reading period for children. Children who are the same age are grouped by ability for their ninety-minute reading block. Reading groups typically have fifteen to twenty children. Placing children into groups ensures everyone's participation and learning. Children are able to discuss their reading and the subject matter, share questions, and seek answers. Educators constantly monitor children's progress, formally and informally. Children are assessed every eight to nine weeks, at which time they receive additional tutoring or are moved to another reading group.

SFA also serves as the reading, writing, and language arts component for Reading Roots and Reading Wings. Reading Roots is an SFA reading program that is introduced in the second semester of kindergarten and is a kindergarten through first-grade reading program. Reading Roots is researched-based and provides a strong foundation for successful reading through systematic phonics instruction supported by decodable stories, along with instruction in fluency and comprehension. Reading Roots also provides rich literature experiences, extensive oral-language development, and thematically focused writing instructions. Children are evaluated and regrouped every quarter according to their reading level to make certain they receive the most focused instruction.

Reading Wings is the SFA reading program designed for children starting in the second grade. Reading Wings teaches strategies for reading, extends reading comprehension skills, enhances written expression, promotes oral-language proficiency, develops fluency, improves listening-comprehension learning, and encourages cooperative learning. A Reading Wings reading block consists of reading with a partner, identifying story details, writing a few paragraphs on a related topic, practicing words orally for vocabulary lessons, retelling a story, and practicing spelling with a peer.

A comprehension test is given to children after three class lessons to assess how well they understood what they read. Educators use the data from assessments to plan lessons or interventions for individual children or groups. Educators also conduct periodic regrouping for children based on their performance at eight-week intervals.

One-on-one tutoring is provided for children who require additional assistance. Tutors are certified educators, but occasionally well-qualified paraprofessionals also tutor children with less-severe reading problems. Research reveals that paraprofessionals are able to teach effectively in early intervention programs if they receive the appropriate professional development, which includes the opportunity to work with highly experienced, trained professionals with a background in reading instruction in early intervention.

Parental involvement is an essential part of success for SFA. Family Support Teams usually consist of at least one parent, a counselor, facilitator, and any other staff member who has a desire to join. The Family Support Team works to establish and maintain good relations with parents and caregivers.

SFA uses a full-time SFA facilitator and an advisory committee. Every school must appoint an educator to act as a facilitator who works with other educators and staff in making sure the program is implemented in the best manner. The advisory committee comprises the administrator of the school, the facilitator educator, and parent representatives who meet regularly to review the program's progress.

The SFA program requires that educators vote whether to implement the program in their school. Professional development in SFA starts with three consecutive days of in-service training before the program is launched. In addition, SFA consultants visit an SFA school for three two-day visits during the school year to work with the administrators, educators, and facilitators.

Researchers and educators have differing conclusions about the success of the SFA program; however, the results from evaluations of several SFA schools in several states reveal that the program increases children's reading performance. In addition, researchers have found SFA to be effective. Educators endorse reading programs that involve a comprehensive approach that includes children, parents, and caregivers, with the goal of ensuring that children read at grade level.

In today's classroom of various cultures, ethnicity, socioeconomic status, and intellectual abilities, the most important program to implement is the one that works for that particular school. No single intervention program succeeds with all children. All reading programs, no matter how comprehensive, must be supported by the instruction that children receive as part of their regular classroom program. In addition, in order to prevent reading difficulties, educators must monitor children and give them targeted supports as soon as they begin to fall behind their age levels. Furthermore, educators must enlighten parents and caregivers of the significant impact early-intervention programs have on helping their children learn to read.

SUPPLEMENTAL COMPREHENSIVE INTERVENTION READING PROGRAMS

There are several supplemental comprehensive intervention reading programs (CIRP) for the primary grades. CIRP guide more intensive instruction in all five of the essential components of reading instruction: phonemic awareness, phonics, fluency, vocabulary, and comprehension. These programs are intended for children who are reading one or more years below grade level and who are experiencing difficulties with a broad range of reading skills. Instruction provided through these programs accelerates growth in reading with the goal of making children acquire grade-level proficiency. The following is a list of CIRP:

Name of Program	Grade Reviewed
Accelerated Literacy Learning (A.L.L.)	1
Breakthrough to Literacy	K–3
Destination Reading	K–3
Direct Instruction (DI)	K–5
Early Success	1–2
Earobics	K–3
First Grade Peer-Assisted Literacy Strategies	1
FOCUS Reading and Language Program	K–3
Fundations	K–3
Funnix Reading Programs	K–2
Harcourt Trophies First Grade Intervention Kit	1
Headsprout Early Reading	K–2
iStation	K–3
Lightspan Early Reading Program	K–3
Lindamood Phoneme Sequencing (LiPS)	K–3
Open Court	K–6
PLATO Early Reading Program	K–3
PLATO FOCUS and Reading Language Program	K–3
Read, Write & Type! Learning System	1–3
Reading Horizons	K–3
Reading Rescue	1
Saxon Phonics and Spelling	K–3
Sing, Spell, Read and Write	K–2
Voyager Passport	K

In addition to these supplemental CIRP, a well-known program that is widely used in kindergarten through grade twelve is Accelerated Reader (AR)/Reading Renaissance, a software assessment that is a motivational program for the practice of reading. The AR software administers reading quizzes for class-wide use. Quizzes provide individualized information about children's progress and challenges, facilitating educators' feedback to children, parents, caregivers, and other school personnel.

After reading a selected book, a child takes a computerized reading quiz. Quizzes consist of multiple-choice questions to assess the child's comprehension of the book. The quizzes may contain five, ten, or twenty questions, with the number of questions increasing with the child's reading level. Children in lower elementary are expected to receive scores of 85 percent or greater on quizzes; however, individual schools may set different passing grades. Passing the quiz indicates that the child understood what he or she read. Educators use the quiz results to help children set goals and to direct ongoing reading practice. AR meets children's learning needs in the essential components of reading instruction—phonemic awareness, phonics, fluency, vocabulary, and comprehension.

Educators must inform parents and caregivers that they can search online at AR Bookfinder (http://www.arbookfind.com/) for books of interest for their children and see a brief description of the book and the book level. Book titles can be searched based on authors, topics, or titles of books. Many children benefit from the added instruction and practice from the AR program. Some schools use AR to offer incentives such as books or pizza parties for children who achieve a certain number of points through their reading.

ACTION STEPS FOR EDUCATORS

The ability to read is a child's civil right; nevertheless, many children lack the reading skills to place them at proficient levels. Research indicates that educators need to consider the following:

- As early as possible, evaluate each child's developing reading ability and determine appropriate interventions.
- Support high-quality professional development in research-based instruction that allows sufficient time for educators to train and support each other.
- Seek opportunities to consult with knowledgeable and experienced reading specialists to discuss ongoing school-wide strategies for literacy improvement.
- Implement research-based strategies to promote a school-wide focus on literacy, including allocating extended blocks of time to reading in the early grades.
- Find ways to increase one-on-one reading between children and adults by recruiting volunteers or dispatching staff members during the school day, after school, and during the summer.
- Develop relationships with community organizations and private industry for help in providing high-quality professional development.
- Promote independent reading at least thirty minutes a day. Provide children, parents, and caregivers with specific reading assignments, age-appropriate reading lists, and home assignments, linked to classwork, that involve parental involvement.

- Teach children whose first language is not English to read in their native language if instructional guides, learning materials, and locally available proficient educators are available.
- Encourage parents and caregivers to stay involved in their children's education.
- Encourage open communication between home and school to enhance a child's progress and success.
- Contact local libraries, literacy groups, businesses, and community members to provide children who are experiencing reading difficulties with high-quality, after-school, and summer learning opportunities that support and encourage literacy development. See appendix I for a list of resources on literacy and reading for everyone to use.

POINTS TO REMEMBER

Substantial research exists for implementing effective interventions for children with reading difficulties in the elementary grades. These interventions sometimes include the Reading Recovery (RR), Response to Intervention (RTI or RtI) models, and the Success for All (SFA) programs. These programs help educators identify children in need of intervention and implement evidence-based intervention to promote their reading success. Experts have found that with prevention and early intervention, reading failure in the early years is reduced to less than one in ten children. Well-trained educators and reading instructions based on research deliver the best teaching strategies and programs to all children. To transform early learners into superb readers, professional development must be perceived as one of the primary vehicles to bring about change. Professional development for educators is crucial for the success of any reading program. Like children, educators and administrators are also lifelong learners.

Effectiveness in the early grades comes from boosting and fostering motivation, which can strengthen intellectual curiosity and promote more vigorous learning in early learners. Motivation is directly related to a child's success in school. Educators must reward diligence during the early grades as a way to encourage children to strive for their best. Nevertheless, in the primary grades, children with reading difficulties may need intervention to prevent future reading failure. Early recognition of children who need intervention has become a key factor in the prevention of reading difficulties.

Certainly the ability to read proficiently is not only critical to every child's success in today's society, but also his or her right. Because the foundation for reading skills is established during a child's early years, positive early literacy experiences are necessary to help children become proficient readers. Educators, parents, caregivers, and communities across the nation must share the responsibility of ensuring that every child becomes a proficient reader. Also, the improvement of children's reading skills must remain a top priority for leaders at all levels of government and businesses, as well as parents, caregivers, educators, and community members who volunteer to teach reading in programs across the nation.

Nothing that is done for children is ever wasted. All high-quality time spent with children fosters in them the confidence to explore their world. By enlisting the human resources inherent in every school, home, and community, every child can be ensured the opportunity of learning to read. Together, all concerned individuals must transform education for the benefit of all children, which enables them to understand the power of words and how words enrich their lives. Through reading, children are best able to understand the world. As society becomes more technically and socially complex, early learners must not miss out on the fundamentals of reading. It is crucial to educate children in their early years so they can acquire power to magnify themselves and strive for nothing less than excellence.

QUOTATION: TEACHERS AND TEACHING

An understanding heart is everything in a teacher, and cannot be esteemed highly enough. One looks back with appreciation to the brilliant teachers, but with gratitude to those who touched our human feeling. The curriculum is so much necessary raw material, but warmth is the vital element for the growing plant and for the soul of the child.

Carl Gustav Jung, Swiss psychologist (1875–1961)

Appendix A

High-Frequency Words 1–100

the	of	and	a	to	in	is	you	that	it
he	for	was	on	are	as	with	his	they	at
be	this	from	I	have	or	by	one	had	not
but	what	all	were	when	we	there	can	an	your
which	their	said	if	do	will	each	about	how	up
out	them	then	she	many	some	so	these	would	other
into	has	more	her	two	like	him	see	time	could
no	make	than	first	been	its	who	now	people	my
made	over	did	down	only	way	find	use	may	water
long	little	very	after	words	called	just	where	most	know

Appendix B

Lists of 300
Instant Sight Words

FIRST HUNDRED INSTANT SIGHT WORDS

(Fry and Kress, 2006)

a	can	her	many	see	us
about	come	here	me	she	very
after	day	him	much	so	was
again	did	his	my	some	we
all	do	how	new	take	were
an	down	I	no	that	what
and	eat	if	not	the	when
any	for	in	of	their	which
are	from	is	old	them	who
as	get	it	on	then	will
at	give	just	one	there	with
be	go	know	or	they	work
been	good	like	other	this	would
before	had	little	our	three	you
boy	has	long	out	to	your
but	have	make	put	two	
by	he	man	said	up	

Appendix B

SECOND HUNDRED INSTANT SIGHT WORDS

(Fry and Kress, 2006)

also	color	home	must	red	think
am	could	house	name	right	too
another	dear	into	near	run	tree
away	each	kind	never	saw	under
back	ear	last	next	say	until
ball	end	leave	night	school	upon
because	far	left	only	seem	use
best	find	let	open	shall	want
better	first	live	over	should	way
big	five	look	own	soon	where
black	found	made	people	stand	while
book	four	may	play	such	white
both	friend	men	please	sure	wish
box	girl	more	present	tell	why
bring	got	morning	pretty	than	year
call	hand	most	ran	these	
came	high	mother	read	thing	

THIRD HUNDRED INSTANT SIGHT WORDS

(Fry and Kress, 2006)

along	didn't	food	keep	sat	though
always	does	full	letter	second	today
anything	dog	funny	longer	set	took
around	don't	gave	love	seven	town
ask	door	goes	might	show	try
ate	dress	green	money	sing	turn
bed	early	grow	myself	sister	walk
brown	eight	hat	now	sit	warm
buy	every	happy	o'clock	six	wash
car	eyes	hard	off	sleep	water
carry	face	head	once	small	woman
clean	fall	hear	order	start	write
close	fast	help	pair	stop	yellow
clothes	fat	hold	part	ten	yes
coat	fine	hope	ride	thank	yesterday
cold	fire	hot	round	third	
cut	fly	jump	same	those	

Appendix C

Alphabet Chart

Aa - Apple	Ss - Sun
Bb - Bat	Tt - Turtle
Cc - Cat	Uu - Umbrella
Dd - Dog	Vv - Violin
Ee - Egg	Ww - Window
Ff - Fish	Xx - X-ray
Gg - Gift	Yy - Yo-yo
Hh - Hat	Zz - Zipper
Ii - Igloo	
Jj - Jet	
Kk - Kite	
Ll - Lion	
Mm - Monkey	
Nn - Nest	
Oo - Octopus	
Pp - Pizza	
Qq - Queen	
Rr - Rocket	

Appendix D

Digraph and
Blend Sounds Charts

Digraphs are two letters, that, when placed side by side, create a new sound.

ch	wh
sh	ph
th	gh

The following words contain digraphs (notice that *th* has two sounds):

chair	share	them	throw	when	phone
chin	shop	this	thing	where	photo
chomp	shell	there	thin	why	rough
church	ship	then	thumb	what	

BLEND SOUNDS CHART

br - bread	cr - cry	dr - drum	fr - frog	gr - grass	pr- pretzel
tr - tree	wr - wrist	bl - block	cl - clock	fl - flag	gl - glass
pl - plant	sl - slide	sc - scale	sk - skate	sm - smile	sn - snake
sp - spoon	st - star	sw - swim	tw - twenty	sh - shoe	th - thumb
wh - whistle	ch - chair				

Appendix E

Silent *E* Chart

Have children read each word. Then have them add a silent *e* to each card and read the new word.

bit	e
can	e
tap	e
not	e
tub	e
hat	e
hid	e
pet	e
strip	e
scrap	e
glob	e
mad	e
hop	e
rip	e
pal	e
slid	e

Appendix F

Educational Literacy Websites

AUDIOBOOKCLOUD

This is an online streaming audio book collection geared toward public libraries; however, elementary educators can sign up for a free trial. A free, no-obligation, thirty-day trial allows any individual in a particular school or library unlimited access to the complete AudioBookCloud collection. Unlimited remote access makes the collection accessible from home.
http://www.audiobookcloud.com

COLORÍN COLORADO

This website provides useful information, activities, and resources for educators of English Language Learners (ELL) and Spanish speaking parents, and caregivers. Many of their activities are designed for children in pre-kindergarten through grade three.
http://www.colorincolorado.org/

COMPACT FOR READING GUIDE AND SCHOOL-HOME LINKS READING KITS

These are designed to improve reading and other language art skills of children from kindergarten through third grade, including children with disabilities and limited English proficiency. The Compact for Reading

Guide offers tips on creating community and school-family partnerships with the purpose of improving children's reading. The School-Home Links Reading Kits are a collection of research-based activities designed to help families reinforce their children's reading and language arts skills that they learn at school. The School-Home Links Reading Kits are available in Spanish.

  http://www2.ed.gov/pubs/CompactforReading/

CURIOUS GEORGE GAMES AND ACTIVITIES

These are fun-filled interactive games and printable fun activities for children ages three and up.

  http://www.houghtonmifflinbooks.com/features/cgsite/games.shtml

FAMILY EDUCATION NETWORK

The company's mission is to be an online consumer network of the world's best learning and information resources, personalized to help children of all ages take control of their learning and make it part of their everyday lives.

  http://www.familyeducation.com

FREEREADING

This is a high-quality, open-source, free reading-intervention program for pre-kindergarten through grade six. FreeReading contains activities and intervention materials for the following early literacy skills—phonological awareness, phonics, comprehension, vocabulary, fluency, and writing.

  http://www.free-reading.net/index.php?title=Main_Page

FUNBRAIN

This is a popular online website for interactive and educational games, online books, and comics for children of all ages. The playground on the website helps introduce children to the Internet and teaches them how to manipulate the mouse and keyboard.

  http://www.funbrain.com/

KIDSREADS

This website is designed for children ages six and up. It contains information about children's books and authors from the classics to brand-new titles, and some related games. The books on this website are categorized by age and genre.
http://www.kidsreads.com/

MAMAMEDIA

This is a multimedia website designed to foster digital literacy skills for children. Children learn to invent, make, and share their own puzzles, stories, cartoons, polls, quizzes, and more. In addition, there are easy-to-follow lesson plans and tutorials for educators, parents, and caregivers who have little or no previous experiences with computers, the Internet, and programmable media technology.
http://www.Mamamedia.com

ONECLICKDIGITAL

This website provides access to a variety of books in a downloadable e-audio format. Books can be listened to on a computer or transferred to a digital device.
http://www.oneclickaudio.com

PUBLIC BROADCASTING SERVICE (PBS) FOR KIDS

This is a website where children can play educational games and activities. PBS for Kids games are research-based and are designed to foster early learning.
http://pbskids.org/

PUBLIC BROADCASTING SERVICE (PBS) FOR PARENTS

This website is filled with information about children's development from birth through the early school years. It contains guides on a variety of topics, such as reading, language milestones, and child development tracker on literacy. Age-appropriate books can be found by using the book finder on the website. The guide is available in Spanish—*Bienvenidos a PBS Padres*.
http://www.pbs.org/parents/

READING GAME

This website offers free programmed reading lessons geared toward children pre-kindergarten through third grade. The Montessori Home produces the Reading Game. It is based on proven Montessori educational principles that encourage children to focus on the learning opportunity without needless distractions.

http://www.learntoreadfree.com

READING ROCKETS

This is a national multimedia literacy initiative funded by the U.S. Department of Education The website provides research-based strategies, best-practice, and resources on how children learn to read, why they struggle, and how caring adults can help. Reading Rockets also produces award-winning television programs for national broadcast on PBS. Reading Rockets uses the power of television to show how parents and educators can help children become better readers.

http://www.readingrockets.org/

SCHOLASTIC

This website contains age-appropriate guides for helping children from pre-kindergarten to twelfth grade. The website contains resources that help children with reading and other subjects such as language arts, math, science, and social studies. The formats include books, audio, video and software, games, classroom materials, and instructional programs.

http://www.scholastic.com/

STARFALL

This is a website that provides a variety of early literacy activities to teach children to read with phonics, in conjunction with phonemic awareness practice. Starfall is designed for children from pre-kindergarten to grade three, including special education, home schoolers, English language learners, and struggling readers.

http://www.starfall.com/

STORYPLACE

This is an interactive website that provides the virtual experience of going to the library and participating in the same types of activities the library

offers. Children can listen to interactive stories, play with online activities, print take-home activities and reading lists. This website is available in English and Spanish.
http://www.storyplace.org

TIME FOR KIDS (TFK)

This is a division magazine of *Time* magazine. It is a news magazine produced especially for children in grades kindergarten through sixth grade. This website offers age-appropriate news stories and shares diverse resources for kids including virtual tours around the world, homework help, and games.
http://www.timeforkids.com

TUMBLEBOOKLIBRARY

This website is one of the best sites for interactive read-along stories. It furnishes an online collection of animated, talking picture books that engage and draw a child's interest, and are attractively illustrated. In addition, there are reading comprehension quizzes, educational games, and teacher resources for libraries. The TumbleBookLibrary collection can be accessed online from any computer in a school or library with Internet connection, or from home through a direct link on a child's school or library website. TumbleBooks may also be downloaded with TumbleBooks UNPLUGGED application, and there is no Internet required to view books. The TumbleBooks language drop down menu allows users to view the entire website in Spanish or French.
http://www.tumblebooks.com

TUMBLEREADABLES

This is an online collection of read-along titles for elementary and upper-level school children that features online text and complete narration. Sentences are highlighted as they are read and the pages turn automatically. Titles can also be viewed in three different text sizes. TumbleReadables are great for emergent, struggling, and reluctant readers, as well as an excellent tool for English as a Second Language (ESL). TumbleReadables can be enjoyed by accomplished readers who can follow along to the narration of their favorite books.
http://www.TumbleReadables.com

AN INFORMATIVE WEBSITE

Children's Technology Review

120 Main Street, Flemington, NJ 08822
Phone: 1-800-993-9499
This is a monthly newsletter—modeled in the spirit of *Consumer Reports*—designed to summarize products and trends in children's interactive media.
   http://www.childrenstech.com

Appendix G

Newbery Medal Books (1922–2012)

2012: *Dead End in Norvelt* by Jack Gantos (Farrar, Straus & Giroux)

2011: *Moon over Manifest* by Clare Vanderpool (Delacorte Press, an imprint of Random House Children's Books)

2010: *When You Reach Me* by Rebecca Stead (Wendy Lamb Books, an imprint of Random House Children's Books)

2009: *The Graveyard Book* by Neil Gaiman, illustrated by Dave McKean (HarperCollins)

2008: *Good Masters! Sweet Ladies! Voices from a Medieval Village* by Laura Amy Schlitz (Candlewick)

2007: *The Higher Power of Lucky* by Susan Patron, illustrated by Matt Phelan (Simon & Schuster / Richard Jackson)

2006: *Criss Cross* by Lynne Rae Perkins (Greenwillow Books / HarperCollins)

2005: *Kira-Kira* by Cynthia Kadohata (Atheneum Books for Young Readers / Simon & Schuster)

2004: *The Tale of Despereaux: Being the Story of a Mouse, a Princess, Some Soup, and a Spool of Thread* by Kate DiCamillo (Candlewick Press)

2003: *Crispin: The Cross of Lead* by Avi (Hyperion Books for Children)

2002: *A Single Shard* by Linda Sue Park (Clarion Books / Houghton Mifflin)

2001: *A Year Down Yonder* by Richard Peck (Dial)

2000: *Bud, Not Buddy* by Christopher Paul Curtis (Delacorte)

1999: *Holes* by Louis Sachar (Frances Foster)

1998: *Out of the Dust* by Karen Hesse (Scholastic)

1997: *The View from Saturday* by E. L. Konigsburg (Jean Karl / Atheneum)

1996: *The Midwife's Apprentice* by Karen Cushman (Clarion)

1995: *Walk Two Moons* by Sharon Creech (HarperCollins)

1994: *The Giver* by Lois Lowry (Houghton)
1993: *Missing May* by Cynthia Rylant (Jackson/Orchard)
1992: *Shiloh* by Phyllis Reynolds Naylor (Atheneum)
1991: *Maniac Magee* by Jerry Spinelli (Little, Brown)
1990: *Number the Stars* by Lois Lowry (Houghton)
1989: *Joyful Noise: Poems for Two Voices* by Paul Fleischman (Harper)
1988: *Lincoln: A Photobiography* by Russell Freedman (Clarion)
1987: *The Whipping Boy* by Sid Fleischman (Greenwillow)
1986: *Sarah, Plain and Tall* by Patricia MacLachlan (Harper)
1985: *The Hero and the Crown* by Robin McKinley (Greenwillow)
1984: *Dear Mr. Henshaw* by Beverly Cleary (Morrow)
1983: *Dicey's Song* by Cynthia Voigt (Atheneum)
1982: *A Visit to William Blake's Inn: Poems for Innocent and Experienced Travelers* by Nancy Willard (Harcourt)
1981: *Jacob Have I Loved* by Katherine Paterson (Crowell)
1980: *A Gathering of Days: A New England Girl's Journal, 1830–1832* by Joan W. Blos (Scribner)
1979: *The Westing Game* by Ellen Raskin (Dutton)
1978: *Bridge to Terabithia* by Katherine Paterson (Crowell)
1977: *Roll of Thunder, Hear My Cry* by Mildred D. Taylor (Dial)
1976: *The Grey King* by Susan Cooper (McElderry/Atheneum)
1975: *M. C. Higgins, the Great* by Virginia Hamilton (Macmillan)
1974: *The Slave Dancer* by Paula Fox (Bradbury)
1973: *Julie of the Wolves* by Jean Craighead George (Harper)
1972: *Mrs. Frisby and the Rats of NIMH* by Robert C. O'Brien (Atheneum)
1971: *Summer of the Swans* by Betsy Byars (Viking)
1970: *Sounder* by William H. Armstrong (Harper)
1969: *The High King* by Lloyd Alexander (Holt)
1968: *From the Mixed-Up Files of Mrs. Basil E. Frankweiler* by E. L. Konigsburg (Atheneum)
1967: *Up a Road Slowly* by Irene Hunt (Follett)
1966: *I, Juan de Pareja* by Elizabeth Borton de Trevino (Farrar)
1965: *Shadow of a Bull* by Maia Wojciechowska (Atheneum)
1964: *It's Like This, Cat* by Emily Neville (Harper)
1963: *A Wrinkle in Time* by Madeleine L'Engle (Farrar)
1962: *The Bronze Bow* by Elizabeth George Speare (Houghton)
1961: *Island of the Blue Dolphins* by Scott O'Dell (Houghton)
1960: *Onion John* by Joseph Krumgold (Crowell)
1959: *The Witch of Blackbird Pond* by Elizabeth George Speare (Houghton)
1958: *Rifles for Watie* by Harold Keith (Crowell)
1957: *Miracles on Maple Hill* by Virginia Sorensen (Harcourt)
1956: *Carry On, Mr. Bowditch* by Jean Lee Latham (Houghton)
1955: *The Wheel on the School* by Meindert DeJong (Harper)

1954: . . . *And Now Miguel* by Joseph Krumgold (Crowell)
1953: *Secret of the Andes* by Ann Nolan Clark (Viking)
1952: *Ginger Pye* by Eleanor Estes (Harcourt)
1951: *Amos Fortune, Free Man* by Elizabeth Yates (Dutton)
1950: *The Door in the Wall* by Marguerite de Angeli (Doubleday)
1949: *King of the Wind* by Marguerite Henry (Rand McNally)
1948: *The Twenty-One Balloons* by William Pène du Bois (Viking)
1947: *Miss Hickory* by Carolyn Sherwin Bailey (Viking)
1946: *Strawberry Girl* by Lois Lenski (Lippincott)
1945: *Rabbit Hill* by Robert Lawson (Viking)
1944: *Johnny Tremain* by Esther Forbes (Houghton)
1943: *Adam of the Road* by Elizabeth Janet Gray (Viking)
1942: *The Matchlock Gun* by Walter Edmonds (Dodd)
1941: *Call It Courage* by Armstrong Sperry (Macmillan)
1940: *Daniel Boone* by James Daugherty (Viking)
1939: *Thimble Summer* by Elizabeth Enright (Rinehart)
1938: *The White Stag* by Kate Seredy (Viking)
1937: *Roller Skates* by Ruth Sawyer (Viking)
1936: *Caddie Woodlawn* by Carol Ryrie Brink (Macmillan)
1935: *Dobry* by Monica Shannon (Viking)
1934: *Invincible Louisa: The Story of the Author of Little Women* by Cornelia Meigs (Little, Brown)
1933: *Young Fu of the Upper Yangtze* by Elizabeth Lewis (Winston)
1932: *Waterless Mountain* by Laura Adams Armer (Longmans)
1931: *The Cat Who Went to Heaven* by Elizabeth Coatsworth (Macmillan)
1930: *Hitty, Her First Hundred Years* by Rachel Field (Macmillan)
1929: *The Trumpeter of Krakow* by Eric P. Kelly (Macmillan)
1928: *Gay Neck, the Story of a Pigeon* by Dhan Gopal Mukerji (Dutton)
1927: *Smoky, the Cowhorse* by Will James (Scribner)
1926: *Shen of the Sea* by Arthur Bowie Chrisman (Dutton)
1925: *Tales from Silver Lands* by Charles Finger (Doubleday)
1924: *The Dark Frigate* by Charles Hawes (Little, Brown)
1923: *The Voyages of Doctor Dolittle* by Hugh Lofting (Stokes)
1922: *The Story of Mankind* by Hendrik Willem van Loon (Liveright)

Appendix H

Caldecott Medal Books (1938–2012)

2012: *A Ball for Daisy* by Chris Raschka (Schwartz & Wade Books, an imprint of Random House Children's Books, a division of Random House, Incorporated)

2011: *A Sick Day for Amos McGee*, illustrated by Erin E. Stead, written by Philip C. Stead (Neal Porter Books/Roaring Brook Press, an imprint of Macmillan Children's Publishing Group)

2010: *The Lion and the Mouse* by Jerry Pinkney (Little, Brown and Company)

2009: *The House in the Night*, illustrated by Beth Krommes, written by Susan Marie Swanson (Houghton Mifflin Company)

2008: *The Invention of Hugo Cabret* by Brian Selznick (Scholastic Press, an imprint of Scholastic)

2007: *Flotsam* by David Wiesner (Clarion)

2006: *The Hello, Goodbye Window*, illustrated by Chris Raschka, written by Norton Juster (Michael di Capua/Hyperion)

2005: *Kitten's First Full Moon* by Kevin Henkes (Greenwillow Books/HarperCollins Publishers)

2004: *The Man Who Walked between the Towers* by Mordicai Gerstein (Roaring Brook Press/Millbrook Press)

2003: *My Friend Rabbit* by Eric Rohmann (Roaring Brook Press/Millbrook Press)

2002: *The Three Pigs* by David Wiesner (Clarion/Houghton Mifflin)

2001: *So You Want to Be President*, illustrated by David Small; text by Judith St. George (Philomel Books)

2000: *Joseph Had a Little Overcoat* by Simms Taback (Viking)

1999: *Snowflake Bentley*, illustrated by Mary Azarian; text: Jacqueline Briggs Martin (Houghton)
1998: *Rapunzel* by Paul O. Zelinsky (Dutton)
1997: *Golem* by David Wisniewski (Clarion)
1996: *Officer Buckle and Gloria* by Peggy Rathmann (Putnam)
1995: *Smoky Night*, illustrated by David Diaz; text: Eve Bunting (Harcourt)
1994: *Grandfather's Journey* by Allen Say; text: edited by Walter Lorraine (Houghton)
1993: *Mirette on the High Wire* by Emily Arnold McCully (Putnam)
1992: *Tuesday* by David Wiesner (Clarion Books)
1991: *Black and White* by David Macaulay (Houghton)
1990: *Lon Po Po: A Red-Riding Hood Story from China* by Ed Young (Philomel)
1989: *Song and Dance Man*, illustrated by Stephen Gammell; text: Karen Ackerman (Knopf)
1988: *Owl Moon*, illustrated by John Schoenherr; text: Jane Yolen (Philomel)
1987: *Hey, Al*, illustrated by Richard Egielski; text: Arthur Yorinks (Farrar)
1986: *The Polar Express* by Chris Van Allsburg (Houghton)
1985: *Saint George and the Dragon*, illustrated by Trina Schart Hyman; text: retold by Margaret Hodges (Little, Brown)
1984: *The Glorious Flight: Across the Channel with Louis Bleriot* by Alice and Martin Provensen (Viking)
1983: *Shadow*, translated and illustrated by Marcia Brown; original text in French: Blaise Cendrars (Scribner)
1982: *Jumanji* by Chris Van Allsburg (Houghton)
1981: *Fables* by Arnold Lobel (Harper)
1980: *Ox-Cart Man*, illustrated by Barbara Cooney; text: Donald Hall (Viking)
1979: *The Girl Who Loved Wild Horses* by Paul Goble (Bradbury)
1978: *Noah's Ark* by Peter Spier (Doubleday)
1977: *Ashanti to Zulu: African Traditions*, illustrated by Leo and Diane Dillon; text: Margaret Musgrove (Dial)
1976: *Why Mosquitoes Buzz in People's Ears*, illustrated by Leo and Diane Dillon; text: retold by Verna Aardema (Dial)
1975: *Arrow to the Sun* by Gerald McDermott (Viking)
1974: *Duffy and the Devil*, illustrated by Margot Zemach; retold by Harve Zemach (Farrar)
1973: *The Funny Little Woman*, illustrated by Blair Lent; text: retold by Arlene Mosel (Dutton)
1972: *One Fine Day*, retold and illustrated by Nonny Hogrogian (Macmillan)
1971: *A Story A Story*, retold and illustrated by Gail E. Haley (Atheneum)

1970: *Sylvester and the Magic Pebble* by William Steig (Windmill Books)

1969: *The Fool of the World and the Flying Ship*, illustrated by Uri Shulevitz; text: retold by Arthur Ransome (Farrar)

1968: *Drummer Hoff*, illustrated by Ed Emberley; text: adapted by Barbara Emberley (Prentice-Hall)

1967: *Sam, Bangs & Moonshine* by Evaline Ness (Holt)

1966: *Always Room for One More*, illustrated by Nonny Hogrogian; text: Sorche Nic Leodhas, pseudonym [Leclair Alger] (Holt)

1965: *May I Bring a Friend?*, illustrated by Beni Montresor; text: Beatrice Schenk de Regniers (Atheneum)

1964: *Where the Wild Things Are* by Maurice Sendak (Harper)

1963: *The Snowy Day* by Ezra Jack Keats (Viking)

1962: *Once a Mouse*, retold and illustrated by Marcia Brown (Scribner)

1961: *Baboushka and the Three Kings*, illustrated by Nicolas Sidjakov; text: Ruth Robbins (Parnassus)

1960: *Nine Days to Christmas*, illustrated by Marie Hall Ets; text: Marie Hall Ets and Aurora Labastida (Viking)

1959: *Chanticleer and the Fox*, illustrated by Barbara Cooney; text: adapted from Chaucer's *Canterbury Tales* by Barbara Cooney (Crowell)

1958: *Time of Wonder* by Robert McCloskey (Viking)

1957: *A Tree Is Nice*, illustrated by Marc Simont; text: Janice Udry (Harper)

1956: *Frog Went A-Courtin'*, illustrated by Feodor Rojankovsky; text: retold by John Langstaff (Harcourt)

1955: *Cinderella, or the Little Glass Slipper*, illustrated by Marcia Brown; text: translated from Charles Perrault by Marcia Brown (Scribner)

1954: *Madeline's Rescue* by Ludwig Bemelmans (Viking)

1953: *The Biggest Bear* by Lynd Ward (Houghton)

1952: *Finders Keepers*, illustrated by Nicolas, pseudonym [Nicholas Mordvinoff]; text: Will, pseudonym [William Lipkind] (Harcourt)

1951: *The Egg Tree* by Katherine Milhous (Scribner)

1950: *Song of the Swallows* by Leo Politi (Scribner)

1949: *The Big Snow* by Berta and Elmer Hader (Macmillan)

1948: *White Snow, Bright Snow*, illustrated by Roger Duvoisin; text: Alvin Tresselt (Lothrop)

1947: *The Little Island*, illustrated by Leonard Weisgard; text: Golden MacDonald, pseudonym [Margaret Wise Brown] (Doubleday)

1946: *The Rooster Crows* by Maud and Miska Petersham (Macmillan)

1945: *Prayer for a Child*, illustrated by Elizabeth Orton Jones; text: Rachel Field (Macmillan)

1944: *Many Moons*, illustrated by Louis Slobodkin; text: James Thurber (Harcourt)

1943: *The Little House* by Virginia Lee Burton (Houghton)
1942: *Make Way for Ducklings* by Robert McCloskey (Viking)
1941: *They Were Strong and Good* by Robert Lawson (Viking)
1940: *Abraham Lincoln* by Ingri and Edgar Parin d'Aulaire (Doubleday)
1939: *Mei Li* by Thomas Handforth (Doubleday)
1938: *Animals of the Bible, A Picture Book,* illustrated by Dorothy P. Lathrop; text: selected by Helen Dean Fish (Lippincott)

Appendix I

Resources on
Literacy and Reading

AMERICAN LIBRARY ASSOCIATION (ALA)

Association for Library Service to Children (ALSC)
50 East Huron Street, Chicago, IL 60611
Toll-free: 1-800-545-2433, ext. 2163
The ALSC is the world's largest organization dedicated to the support and enhancement of library service to children. The ALSC's network includes children's and youth librarians, children's literature experts, publishers, education and library school faculty members, and other adults dedicated to creating a better future for children through libraries.
  http://www.ala.org/alsc/

CENTER FOR THE IMPROVEMENT
OF EARLY READING ACHIEVEMENT (CIERA)

University of Michigan School of Education
610 East University Ave., Room 1111 SEB, Ann Arbor, MI 48109-1259
Phone: 734-647-6940
CIERA is a national center for research on early childhood reading, representing a grouping of educators from five universities (University of Michigan, Michigan State University, University of Southern California, University of Minnesota, and University of Georgia); other educators; publishers of texts, tests, and technology; professional organizations; schools and school districts across the United States. CIERA is funded

by the U.S. Department of Education, and its mission is to improve the reading achievement of America's children by developing and offering solutions to persistent problems in the learning and teaching of beginning reading.
http://www.ciera.org

COUNCIL FOR EXCEPTIONAL CHILDREN (CEC)

2900 Crystal Dr., Suite 1000, Arlington, VA 22202-3557
Toll-free: 866-509-0218 or Local: 703-620-3660
The CEC is the largest international professional organization dedicated to the educational success of individuals with disabilities and/or gifts and talents. Its audience consists of educators, administrators, children, parents, paraprofessionals, and related support service providers.
http://www.cec.sped.org/AM/Template.cfm?Section=About_CEC

EDUCATION RESOURCES INFORMATION CENTER (ERIC)

Toll-free: 1-800-LET-ERIC (1-800-538-3742)
ERIC is an online digital library of education research and information. ERIC is supported by the Institute of Education Sciences (IES) of the U.S. Department of Education. ERIC provides ready access to education literature to support the use of educational research and information to improve practice in learning, teaching, educational decision making, and research.
http://www.eric.ed.gov/

EVEN START FAMILY LITERACY PROGRAM

U.S. Department of Education, Office of Elementary and Secondary Education
400 Maryland Ave. SW, Washington, DC 20202
Toll-free: 1-800-USA-LEARN (1-800-872-5327)
Even Start provides support for family-centered education projects to help parents learn the literacy and parenting skills they need to help their young children reach their full potential as learners. Even Start makes grants to local education agencies, community-based organizations, and other nonprofit organizations.
http://www.ed.gov/programs/evenstartformula/index.html

INSTITUTE OF EDUCATION SCIENCES
(IES)—WHAT WORKS CLEARINGHOUSE (WWC)

555 New Jersey Ave. NW, Washington, DC 20208
Phone: 202-219-1385
The IES was created as part of the Education Sciences Reform Act of 2002, and as an initiative of the U.S. Department of Education, the WWC was created to be a central and trusted source of scientific evidence for what works in education. IES is the successor of the Office of Educational Research and Improvement (OERI). The mission of the IES is to provide rigorous evidence on which to ground education practice and policy and share the information broadly. The IES identifies what works, what does not and why, and aims to improve educational outcomes for all children, particularly those at risk of failure. The IES is divided into four major research and statistics centers:

1. National Center for Education Statistics (NCES)—conducts the National Assessment of Educational Progress (known as The Nation's Report Card).
2. National Center for Education Research (NCER)
3. National Center for Education Evaluation and Regional Assistance (NCEE)—operates the National Library of Education and the Education Resources Information Center (ERIC).
4. National Center for Special Education Research (NCSER)
   http://ies.ed.gov/

INTERNATIONAL READING ASSOCIATION (IRA)

800 Barksdale Rd., P.O. Box 8139, Newark, DE 19714-8139
Phone: 302-731-1600
The IRA is an organization of educators, librarians, researchers, parents, and caregivers who are dedicated to promoting high levels of literacy for everyone. IRA's online bookstore offers books, videos, and software for parents and caregivers. IRA also publishes three professional journals:

1. *The Reading Teacher*—for individuals working with children to age twelve
2. *Journal of Adolescent & Adult Literacy*—for educators of upper-level school children
3. *Reading Research Quarterly*—publishes contributions in literacy research

The Reading Online is an e-journal sponsored by the organization; it contains hundreds of articles and is available online at http://www .readingonline.org

The association's main website is located at: http://www.reading.org/

LEARNING DISABILITIES ASSOCIATION (LDA) OF AMERICA

4156 Library Rd., Pittsburgh, PA 15234-1349
Toll-free: 1-800-300-6710 or Local: 412-341-1515
The LDA provides support to individuals with learning disabilities and their parents, educators, and other professionals. The LDA provides advanced information on learning disabilities, practical solutions, and a comprehensive network of resources at the national, state, and local levels. These services make the LDA the leading resource for information on learning disabilities.

http://www.ldanatl.org/

NATIONAL ASSOCIATION FOR
THE EDUCATION OF YOUNG CHILDREN (NAEYC)

1313 L St. NW, Suite 500, Washington, DC 20005
Toll-free: 800-424-2460 or 866-NAEYC-4U or Local: 202-232-8777
The NAEYC is the leading membership association for individuals working with and on behalf of children from birth through age eight. NAEYC's members are educators, administrators, parents, policymakers, and others committed to bringing high-quality education and early care to young children. These members are organized in a vibrant network of local, state, and regional affiliate groups.

http://www.naeyc.org/

NATIONAL CENTER FOR FAMILY LITERACY (NCFL)

Waterfront Plaza, Suite 300, 325 West Main St., Louisville, KY 40202-4251
Toll-free: 1-877-326-5481 or Local: 502-584-1133
The NCFL inspires and engages families in the pursuit of education and learning together. NCFL works to strengthen and broaden its approaches to family literacy, by strengthening parent-child confidence, increasing their ability, and broadening their outlook.

http://www.famlit.org

NATIONAL CENTER FOR LEARNING DISABILITIES (NCLD)

381 Park Ave. South, Suite 1401, New York, NY 10016
Toll-free: 1-888-575-7373 or Local: 212-545-7510
The NCLD is a national nonprofit organization that is committed to improving the lives of those affected by learning disabilities. The NCLD provides materials designed to increase public awareness and understanding.
http://www.ncld.org

NATIONAL EARLY CHILDHOOD TECHNICAL ASSISTANCE CENTER (NECTAC)

517 S. Greensboro St., Carrboro, NC 27510
Phone: 919-962-2001
The NECTAC is the national early childhood technical assistance center supported by the U.S. Department of Education's Office of Special Education Programs (OSEP) under the provisions of the IDEA. Under the website's Complete List of Topical Web Pages is a section for emerging literacy that provides information on early literacy for children.
http://www.nectac.org/

NATIONAL INFORMATION CENTER FOR CHILDREN AND YOUTH WITH DISABILITIES (NICHCY)

P.O. Box 1492, Washington, DC 20013-1492
Toll-free: 1-800-695-0285
The NICHCY provides referrals and information on disabilities and related issues for educators, families, and other professionals, with a focus on children and youth (birth to age twenty-two). The NICHCY also provides information on special education and the law through various federal special laws that affect children with disabilities, such as the IDEA.
http://www.nichcy.org

NO CHILD LEFT BEHIND (NCLB) ACT AND ELEMENTARY AND SECONDARY EDUCATION ACT (ESEA)

Toll-free: 1-800-USA-LEARN (1-800-872-5327)
400 Maryland Ave. SW, Washington, DC 20202
Information can be obtained on the NCLB, including the Act and the Obama administration's blueprint for reauthorizing the ESEA:

- ESEA Page—Reauthorizing the ESEA
- ESEA Flexibility—Waivers from No Child Left Behind
- ESEA Blueprint for Reform—Blueprint to ESEA reauthorization
- NCLB Legislation—Public Law PL 107-110, the No Child Left Behind Act of 2001
- NCLB Policies—Policy documents sorted by topic

Information from this website is available in English and Spanish.
http://www2.ed.gov/nclb/landing.jhtml

PROLITERACY

1320 Jamesville Ave., 635 James St., Syracuse, NY 13210-2214
Toll-free: 1-888-528-2224 or Local: 315-472-0001
ProLiteracy is an international nonprofit organization based in Syracuse, New York, that supports individuals and programs that help adults learn to read and write. In the United States, ProLiteracy represents community-based volunteer and adult basic education affiliates in all fifty states and the District of Columbia. ProLiteracy accredits programs and supports them with technical assistance and program and professional development services online, in regional trainings, and at an annual conference. ProLiteracy also serves as a supporter for issues related to adult literacy and lifelong learning.
    ProLiteracy's mission is to improve the lives of adults, families, communities, and societies.
    http://www.literacyvolunteers.org/

READING IS FUNDAMENTAL (RIF)

1255 23rd St. NW, Suite 300, Washington, DC 20037 or
P.O. Box 96897, Washington, DC 20090
Toll-free: 1-877-RIF-READ or Local: 202-536-3400
RIF provides children from birth to age eight and their families with new, free books to choose from and make their own. In addition, RIF prepares and motivates children to read by delivering free books and literacy resources to those children and families who need them most. RIF trusts that they can inspire children to be lifelong readers through the power of choice. RIF trains literacy providers, parents, and caregivers to prepare all children to become lifelong readers.
    http://www.rif.org/

U.S. DEPARTMENT OF HEALTH AND HUMAN SERVICES (HHS)

Head Start Program/Early Head Start
Administration for Children and Families
Early Childhood Learning and Knowledge Center (ECLKC)
Washington, DC 20005
Phone: 866-763-6481
Head Start is a federal program that promotes the school readiness of children ages birth to five from low-income families. Head Start programs provide comprehensive services to enrolled children and their families, which include health, nutrition, social services, and other services that are determined necessary by family needs assessments. In addition to education and cognitive development services, Head Start programs provide a learning environment that supports children's growth in

• language and literacy,
• cognition and general knowledge,
• physical development and health,
• social and emotional development, and
• approaches to learning.

Early Head Start programs—modeled after Head Start—provide services to low-income pregnant women and families with infants and toddlers.
http://eclkc.ohs.acf.hhs.gov/hslc/

Bibliography

American Library Association. 2009. The condition of U.S. libraries: School library trends, 1999–2009. Office for Research and Statistics. Retrieved from http://www.ala.org.../library/stats/

———. 2010. Invaluable school "libraries" under attack. Retrieved from http://www.pio.ala.org/visibility?p=1765.

———. 2000. Kids and reading. Retrieved from http://www.ala.org/pio/factsheets/kidsucceed.html.

Anderson, R. C., E. H. Hiebert, J. A. Scott, and I. A. G. Wilkinson. 1985. *Becoming a nation of readers: The report of the commission on reading.* U.S. Department of Education, Champaign-Urbana, IL: Center for the Study of Reading.

Anderson, R. C., P. T. Wilson, and L. G. Fielding. 1988. Growth in reading and how children spend their time outside of school. *Reading Research Quarterly* 23: 285–304. Retrieved from ERIC database (ED275992).

Association for Library Services to Children. 2012. Caldecott Medal winners, 1938–present. Retrieved from http://www.ala.org/alsc/awardsgrants/bookmedia/caldecottmedal/caldecottwinners/caldecottmedal. Used with permission from the American Library Association.

———. 2012. Newbery Medal winners, 1922–present. Retrieved from http://www.ala.org/alsc/awardsgrants/bookmedia/newberymedal/newberywinners/medalwinners. Used with permission from the American Library Association.

Beck, I. L., and C. Juel. 1995. The role of decoding in learning to read. *American Educator* 19(8): 21–25, 39–42.

Beran, M. K. 2004. In defense of memorization. *City Journal.* Retrieved from http://www.city-journal.org/html/14_3_defense_memorization.html.

Boone, R., K. Higgins, A. Notari, and C. S. Stump. 1996. Hypermedia Pre-reading lessons: Learner-centered software for kindergarten. *Journal of Computing in Childhood Education* 7(1/2): 39–70.

133

Children's Book Committee Bank Street College of Education. 2011. *Best children's books of the year*. New York: Teachers College Press.

Cho, K., and D. Choi. 2008. Are read alouds and free reading "natural partners?" An experimental study. *Knowledge Quest* 6(5): 69–73.

Coleman, J. S., E. Campbell, A. Mood, E. Weinfeld, C. Hobson, R. York, and J. McPartland. 1966. *Equity of Educational Opportunity*. U.S. Department of Health, Education, and Welfare. Washington, DC: U.S. Government Printing Office.

Elementary and Secondary School Act of 1965, Pub. L. 89-10, 42 U.S.C. 1471.

Elley, W. B. 1996. Lifting literacy levels in developing countries: Some implications from an IEA study. In V. Greaney (ed.), *Promoting reading in developing countries*. Newark, DE: International Reading Association. Retrieved from ERIC database (ED400527).

Epstein, J. L. 1987. What principals should know about parent involvement. *Principal* 66(3): 6–9.

Florida Center for Reading Research. 2002. Success for All. Retrieved from http://www.fcrr.org/fcrrreports/pdf/success_for_all_report.pdf.

Fry, E. B., and J. E. Kress. 2006. *The reading teacher's book of lists* (5th ed.). San Francisco: Jossey-Bass.

Gambrell, L. B., B. M. Palmer, and R. M. Coding. 1993. *Motivation to read*. Washington, DC: Office of Educational Research and Improvement.

Gillet, J., and C. Temple. 2004. *Understanding reading problems: Assessment and Instruction* (6th ed.—earlier editions published in 1982, 1986, 1990, 1994, and 1998). Boston: Allyn and Bacon. Reprinted by permission of Pearson Education, Inc., Upper Saddle River, NJ.

Hirsh-Pasek, K., and R. Golinkoff. 2004. Getting engaged through reading. *Knowledge Quest* 33(2): 66–68.

Institute for Education Sciences. 2007a. What Works Clearinghouse (WWC) documents Reading Recovery's scientific research base. Retrieved from http://www.readingrecovery.org/reading_recovery/.

———. 2007b. What Works Clearinghouse topic report on beginning reading. Retrieved from http://ies.ed.gov/ncee/wwc/reports/beginning_reading/.

International Reading Association. 2012. Standards 2010: Reading specialist/literacy coach. Retrieved from http://www.reading.org/General/CurrentResearch/Standards/ProfessionalStandards2010/.

Jentes-Mason, R. 2004. The Literacy Edge: *Expanding the vision for literacy and learning: Staff development notebook*. Fresno, CA: Fresno Pacific University.

Jung, C. G. 2010. Quote by Carl Jung on teachers and teaching: Quotation. *Quotations Book*. HighBeam Research. Retrieved from http://www.highbeam.com/doc/1G1-234834454.html.

Lee, J., W. Grigg, and P. Donahue. 2007. *The nation's report card: Reading 2007*. (NCES 2007496.) Washington, DC: National Center for Education Statistics.

Lyon, R. 1997. *Report on learning disabilities research*. Testimony given at the committee on education and the workforce in U.S. House of Representatives, Washington, DC.

Matthew, K. 1996. What do children think of CD-ROM storybooks? *Texas Reading Report* 18(6).

Morrow, L. M., and C. S. Weinstein. 1986. Encouraging voluntary reading: The impact of a literature program on children's use of library centers. *Reading Research Quarterly* 21(3): 330–46. Retrieved from ERIC database (EJ337403).

Moxley, R. A., and B. Warash. 1990–1991. Spelling strategies of three prekindergarten children on the microcomputer. *Journal of Computing in Childhood Education* 2: 47–61.

National Center for Education Statistics, U.S. Department of Education. 2011. *The nation's report card: Reading 2011*. NCES 2012-457. National Center for Education Statistics, Retrieved from ERIC database (ED525544).

———. 2009. *The nation's report card: 2007 at a glance*. NCES 2009-486. National Center for Education Statistics.

National Center for Family Literacy. 2008. *Developing early literacy: Report of the National Early Literacy Panel. A scientific synthesis of early literacy development and implications for intervention.* Washington, DC: National Institute for Literacy.

National Institute of Child Health and Human Development United States. 1995. *The educator's word frequency.* Touchstone Applied Science Associates and New York State Science Technology Foundation.

National Reading Panel. 2000. *Report of the National Reading Panel: Teaching children to read. An evidence-based assessment of the scientific research literature on reading and its implications for reading instruction.* (NIH Publication No. 00-4769.) Washington, DC: National Institutes of Health and Human Development.

National Research Council. 1998. *Preventing reading difficulties in young children.* Washington, DC: National Academy Press.

Nelson-Royes, A. M., and G. L. Reglin. 2011. Evaluating the effects of the reading component of a private after-school tutoring program for urban students. *Illinois Schools Journal* 91(2): 39–59.

Nicolson, R. I., A. J. Fawcett, and M. K. Nicolson. 2000. Evaluation of a computer-based reading intervention in infant and junior schools. *Journal of Research in Reading* 23: 194–209.

No Child Left Behind Act of 2001, Pub L. No. 107–110, 115 Stat. (2002).

Northeast and the Islands Regional Technology in Education Consortium. 2004. Technology and teaching children to read. Retrieved from http://neirtec.org/reading_report/.

Piaget, J. 1926. *The language and thought of the child.* London: Routledge & Kegan Paul.

Rack, J., C. Hulme, M. Snowling, and J. Wightman. 1994. The role of phonology in young children learning to read words: The direct-mapping hypothesis. *Journal of Experimental Child Psychology* 57(1): 42–71. Retrieved from ERIC database (EJ478174).

Reading is Fundamental. 2009. Multicultural Lending Library: Resource guide. Retrieved from http://www.rif.org/assets/documents/RIF_Multicultural_Lending_Library.pdf.

Reading Rockets. 2012. Helping struggling readers. Retrieved from: www.readingrockets.org/helping.

Scholastic. 2010. 2010 kids and family reading report: Turning the digital age. Retrieved from http://scholastic.com/readingreport.

Slavin, R., C. Lake, S. Davis, and N. Madden. 2011. Effective programs for struggling readers: A best-evidence synthesis. *Educational Research Review* 6(1): 1–26.
———. 2009. *Effective programs for struggling Readers: A best evidence synthesis.* Institute of Education Sciences. U.S. Department of Education. Retrieved
from ERIC database (ED527634).
Slavin, R. E., N. A. Madden, L. J. Dolan, B. A. Wasik, S. M. Ross, and L. J. Smith.
1994. Whenever and wherever we choose: The replication of Success for All.
Phi Delta Kappan International 75(8): 639–47. Retrieved from ERIC database
(EJ481335).
Stacey, S., and K. Wheldall, K. 1999. Essential constituents of effective reading
instruction for low progress readers. *Perspectives on Special Education* 8(1): 44–58.
Success for All Foundation. 2011. Success for All. Retrieved from http://www
.successforall.net.
Tomlinson, T. 1992. *Issues in Education: Hard work and high expectations: Moti-
vating students to learn.* Washington, DC: U.S. Department of Education.
Trelease, J. 2006. *The Read-aloud handbook* (6th ed.). New York: Penguin.
Tressell-Cullen, A. 1999. *Starting with the real world: Strategies for developing nonfic-
tion reading and writing, K–8.* Parsippany, NJ: Dominie Press-Pearson Education.
Tunnell, M. O., and J. S. Jacobs. 2000. *Children's literature, briefly* (2nd ed.). Upper
Saddle River, NJ: Pearson Education, Inc.
U.S. Census Bureau. 2009. Census Bureau estimates nearly half of children under
age 5 are minorities. Retrieved from http://www.census.gov/newsroom/
releases/archives/population/cb09-75.html.
U.S. Department of Education. 2009. *Assisting students struggling with reading: Response to Intervention (RtI) and multi-tier intervention in the primary
grades.* National Center for Education Evaluation and Regional Assistance.
Institute of Education Sciences (IES) NCEE 2009-4045.
———. 2005. *Helping your child become a reader.* Office of Communication and
Outreach, Washington, DC.
———. 2009. *The nation's report card: Reading 2009.* Retrieved from http://nces
.ed.gov/nationsreportcard/pdf/main2009/2010458.pdf.
———. 1999. *Start, finish strong: How to help every child become a reader.* Washington, DC: Author.
———. 2006. *What Works Clearinghouse Intervention Report.* Institute of Education Sciences (IES). Retrieved from ERIC database (ED493667).
Veerkamp, M. B., and D. Kamps. 2007. The effects of classwide peer tutoring on
the reading achievement of urban middle schools students. *Education & Treat-
ment of Children* 30(2): 21–51. Retrieved from ERIC database (EJ778089).

Index

academic achievement, 49–50
Accelerated Reader (AR)/Reading
  Renaissance, 95–96
administrators, 83, 84
ALA. *See* American Library Associa-
  tion
alphabet chart, 105
alphabetic principle, 13
American Library Association (ALA),
  62–63
Association for Library Service to
  Children, 62

background knowledge, 33
"Becoming a Nation of Readers," 26
biography, 75–77, 78
books: children's autonomy in selecting, 44; collection means for, 44;
  early learners' most appropriate, 44;
  educator donation of, 43–44; literacy through access to, 42, 45. *See also*
  chapter books; children's literature;
  easy reader books; e-books; fiction
  books; nonfiction books; picture
  books; traditional literature

Caldecott Award, 62, 63

caregivers. *See* parents
Census Bureau, U.S., 8
chapter books, 66–67
child development research, 46–47
child development theory, 61–62
children: biography appeal for, 77;
  books selected by, 44; computers
  used by, 41–42, 46–47, 48, 53–54;
  dropout, 6–7; high-need, 8; high-
  quality time with, 98; internet
  technology used by, 41–42; library
  association for, 62; library knowledge for, 42; listening *versus* reading
  level in, 26; nature of, ages 1-6, 11;
  personal library for, 44; reading
  challenges for non-mainstream, 7–8;
  technology access for, 41; technology as motivation for, 53–55, 58–59
Children's Book Committee, 63
children's literature: award winning,
  62–63, 65; benefits of, 61, 79–80;
  best, for early learners, 62–63;
  biography as, 75–77; chapter books
  in, 66–67; defined, 61; early learners
  and, 61–80; easy reader books in,
  65–66; educator role in selecting, 62;
  fiction in, 69–71; nonfiction books

Literacy First, 82–84
literate or superb reader, 7
literature, children's. *See* children's
   literature

meaning, 17
mental imagery, 19–20
meta-analysis, 16
Mimic Books, 29
modeling, 17–18, 27–28, 39. *See also*
   teacher modeling
motivation, 53–55, 58–59, 86–87, 97
multimedia, 54

National Assessment of Educational
   Progress (NAEP), 1, 5–6
National Center for Education (NCE),
   5–6
National Center for Education Statis-
   tics (NCES), 41–42
National Education Technology Plan, 42
National Institutes of Health, 82–83
National Reading Panel (NRP): educa-
   tor requirements from, 82; effective
   reading components from, 22, 25,
   50–53, 94; findings by, 9–10; moti-
   vation as reading factor from, 53,
   58–59; phonemic awareness study
   by, 16; shared reading recommen-
   dations from, 30
National Research Council (NRC), 86
"Nation's Report Card: Reading 2011"
   (NCE), 5–6
NCE. *See* National Center for Educa-
   tion
NCES. *See* National Center for Educa-
   tion Statistics
NCLB. *See* No Child Left Behind Act
Newbery Award, 62–63
No Child Left Behind Act (NCLB), 9,
   42, 58, 81
nonfiction books, 67–69
NRC. *See* National Research Council
NRP. *See* National Reading Panel

Observation Survey of Early Literacy
   Achievement, 89

Oxford English Dictionary, 45

parents: early learner involvement
   from, 45; guided reading involvement of, 32; homework monitoring
   by, 8, 12; learning and, 1, 7–8, 12–13,
   21, 30, 32, 37–38, 46, 47, 48; as reading facilitators, 34–35; RTI involvement of, 90, 92; SFA involvement
   for, 93. *See also specific topics*
parents, helping struggling readers:
   educator instruction for, 37; evaluation in, 38; steps in, 38
partnerships, parent-teacher: for early
   reader development, 20–21; in
   general reading development, 1,
   7, 8, 10; in guided reading, 32; in
   independent reading, 34, 35; for
   phonemic awareness development,
   16; in reading aloud, 27; in reading
   intervention, 89–90; in RTI, 92; in
   shared reading, 30; for sight word
   development, 12–13; for struggling
   readers, 37–38; in technology learning, 46, 47, 48
phonemes, 13, 15
phonemic awareness: computer activities involving, 50; defined, 9, 15, 22;
   for early learners, 16; NRP study
   on, 16; parent-teacher partnerships
   in, 16; as phonics foundation, 15;
   phonological awareness containing,
   15; practices encouraging, 13–14; at
   preschool, kindergarten, and first
   grade level, 16; for reading prediction, 15; research findings for,
   15–16; struggling readers instruction in, 36
phonics: alphabetic principle in, 13;
   benefits of, 15; computer activities
   for, 50–51; defined, 9, 22; effective
   readers' use of, 25, 39; at first grade
   level, 12; instruction, 13–15; letter-
   sound relationships in, 12; nature
   of, 13, 39; phonemic awareness as
   foundation for, 15; practices encouraging, 13–14; reading intervention

technological reading programs, 54–55
technology: academic achievement
and, 49–50; children motivated
through, 53–55, 58–59; children's
access to, 41; for early learners, 41,
46, 49–55; early learners motivated through, 53–55; educator
instruction in use of, 48–49; NCLB
practices for literacy in, 42, 58;
parent-teacher partnerships for,
46, 47, 48; reading comprehension
enhanced through, 52; reading im-
pacted by, 2, 45, 49; for struggling
readers, 54; teaching influenced
by, 41, 49. *See also* computers;
internet technology
third-grade level, 18–20, 81
traditional literature, 71–75, 76
tutoring, 88, 93
tutoring programs, examples, 88

vocabulary: easy reader books building, 65–66; independent reading
building, 33; reading, 17; reading
dependent on strong, 17; reading

fluency in, 18; types of, 17
vocabulary learning: classifications
of, 17; computer activities for, 51;
at first grade level, 16; as learning
strategy, 16–17; nature of, 9, 22;
as reading predictor, 16; text type
matching in, 17
voluntary reading. *See* independent
reading

websites, 47, 111–16
What Works Clearinghouse, 90
"What Works for Struggling Children," 36–37
whole language reading: alternative
names for, 23; benefits claimed
from, 25; defined, 23–24, 38–39;
difficulties in, 25; history of, 24;
key elements of, 24; phonics combined with, 24, 25; phonics *versus*,
23–25
word recognition: comprehension,
reading fluency, and, 17; in phonics
instruction, 15; for reading comprehension, 9

About the Author

Andrea Nelson-Royes, EdD, is an educator, researcher, author, and parent who has a passionate interest in how children learn to read and how to keep them reading. She holds a doctoral degree in educational and organizational leadership from Nova Southeastern University in Florida. She has been an educational and business consultant and now enjoys a career as a writer and mother of four children. Her articles have appeared in the *Reading Improvement Journal* and *Illinois Schools Journal*. Andrea is married and lives in the southeastern United States with her children and husband. Please visit her website at www.andreanelsonroyes.com.